J Vodoz

An Essay on the Prose of John Milton

J Vodoz

An Essay on the Prose of John Milton

ISBN/EAN: 9783744693066

Printed in Europe, USA, Canada, Australia, Japan

Cover: Foto ©Thomas Meinert / pixelio.de

More available books at **www.hansebooks.com**

AN ESSAY

ON THE

PROSE OF JOHN MILTON.

BY

J. VODOZ.

Winterthur.
Buchdruckerei von G. Binkert.
1895.

WORKS CONSULTED.

———※———

MILTON, The works of John, ed. by J. Mitford,	London,	1863.
MILTON, Four pamphlets on Divorce,	London,	1644—45.
MILTON, John, Areopagitica,	London,	1644.
MILTON, John, Of Education, to Master S. Hartlib,	London,	1642.
MILTON, John, The Reason of Church Government,	London,	1641.
MILTON, John, Of Reformation touching Church Discipline,	London,	1641.
MILTON, John, Of Prelatical Episcopacy,	London,	1641.
MILTON, John, Eikonoklastes,	London,	1649.
MILTON, John, Tenure of Kings and Magistrates,	London,	1649.
BACON, Francis, Advancement of Learning,	London, ·	1605.
HERBERT, Sir Thos, A relation of some years travel, &c.,	London,	1634.
TAYLOR, Jeremy, A discourse concerning prayer,	London,	1646.
TAYLOR, Jeremy, Treatises of the Liberty of prophesying,	London,	1648.
HOBBES, Thos, Human Nature,	London,	1651.
BROWNE, Sir Thos, Hydriotaphia,	London,	1658.
ENGLISH PROSE, from Maundeville to Thackeray, Cam. Ser., ed. by A. Galton,	London,	1888.
SOTHEBY, S. L., Ramblings in the Elucidation of the autograph of Milton,	London,	1861.
HORWOOD, A. J., A common-place book of J. Milton, reproduced by the autotype process from the orig. MS.,	London,	1876.
BULLOKAR, William, Booke at Large, &c.,	London,	1580.
MULCASTER, Richard, The first part of the Elementarie,	London,	1582.
BULLOKAR, John, An English Expositor,	London,	1616.
GIL, Alexander, Logonomia Anglica,	London,	1619.
HEWES, John, A perfect survey of the English tongue,	London,	1624.
BUTLER, Charles, The English Grammar,	Oxford,	1633.
LILY, William, An English Grammar,	London,	1641.
HODGES, Richard, A special help to Orthographie,	London,	1643.
HODGES, Richard, The English Primrose,	London,	1644.
HODGES, Richard, The plainest directions for the true writing of English,	London,	1649.
COOTE, Edward, The English Schoolmaster,	London,	1662.
MIÈGE, Guy, Nouvelle méthode pour apprendre l'Anglois,	London,	1685.
LILY, William, The Royal Grammar,	London,	1685.
LILY, William, The Royal Grammar reformed,	London,	1695.
EARLE, John, English Prose,	London,	1890.
EARLE, John, The Philology of the English tongue,	Oxford,	1873.
JOHNSON, Dr. Sam., Lives of English Poets,	London,	1816.

PATTISON, Mark, Milton, Engl. Men of Letters Ser., London,   1890.
MORLEY, Prof. Henry, First Sketch of E. Literature, London.   1883.
BUFFON, Discours sur le style, (Disc. Académiques), Paris,   1858.
MORRIS, Dr. Rich., Outlines of E. Accidence,   London,   1873.
SWEET, Henry, A new English Grammar I,   Oxford,   1892.
ABBOTT, E. A., A Shakespearian Grammar,   London,   1870.
MASON, C. P., English Grammar,   London,   1879.
ELLIS, J. Alex., On E. E. Pronunciation,   London,   1869—74.
THE WESTMINSTER REVIEW, LXXX,   London,   1871.
THE BOOKSELLER, 3. Oct. Nr.,   London,   1871.

MÄTZNER, Ed., Englische Grammatik,   Berlin,   1860—66.
KÖLBING, Dr. E., Englische Studien, I—XVII,   Heilbronn,   1877—92.
TEN BRINK, B., Ueber Chaucer's Sprache und
     Verskunst,   Leipzig,   1884.
HERRIG'S Archiv, Bd. XXV—XXXV,   Braunschweig.
GASNER, Ernst, Zum Entwicklungsgang der neu-
     englischen Schriftsprache,   Göttingen,   1891.
GOTTSCHALK, Ueber den Gebrauch des Artikels
     in Milton's Paradise Lost,   Halle,   1883.
ROST, Wold., Die Orthographie der I. 4⁰ Ausgabe
     von Milton's Paradise Lost,   Leipzig,   1892.
JÖRSS, Paul, Grammatisches und Stilistisches aus
     Milton's Areopagitica,   Ratzeburg,   1893.
SCHMIDT, Heinr., Milton considered as a political
     writer,   Halle,   1882.
STERN, A., Milton und seine Zeit,   Leipzig,   1879.

INTRODUCTION.

W$_{HEN}$, about the year 1640, Milton was whirled into politics, he ceased to be a poet "soaring in the high region of his fancies, with his garland and singing robes about him," and was brought "to sit below in the cool element of prose,"[1] entering thus into the second period of his life, which Pattison so well characterises as a drama in three acts. "The first discovers him in the calm and peaceful retirement of Horton, of which l'Allegro, Il Penseroso, and Lycidas are the expression. In the second act he is breathing the foul and heated atmosphere of party passion and religious hatred, generating the lurid fires which glare in the battailous canticles of his prose pamphlets.—The three great poems, Paradise Lost, Paradise Regained, and Samson Agonistes, are the utterance of his final period of solitary and Promethean grandeur, when blind, destitute, friendless, he testified of righteousness, temperance, and judgment to come, alone before a fallen world."[2]

The second part of his life as a writer may then be timed from 1641 to the end of the Commonwealth, 1660, and the whole number of his political pamphlets is twenty-five. Of these, twenty-one are written in English, and four in Latin. Nine relate to church government, or ecclesiastical affairs;[3] eight treat of the various crises of the

---

[1] Reason of Church Government. II. Introduction.

[2] M. Pattison. "Milton," Engl. Men of Letters Series, p. 14.

[3] 1. Of Reformation touching Church Discipline in England. May 1641. 2. Of Prelaticall Episcopacy. June 1641. 3. Animadversions upon the Remonstrant's defence against Smectymnuus. July 1641. 4. Reason of Church Government. Febr. 1642. 5. Apology against a pamphlet called a modest confutation. March 1642. 6. A treatise of Civil Power in Ecclesiastical Causes. 1659. 7. Considerations touching the likeliest means to remove Hirelings out of the Church. 1659. 8. Brief notes upon a late Sermon by Dr. Griffiths. 1660. 9. Of true Religion, Heresy and Schism. 1673.

civil strife,[1] and two are personal vindications of himself against one of his antagonists.[2] There remain to be mentioned four pamphlets on divorce, 1643—1645, his tractate:—"Of Education:—to Master Samuel Hartlib" (1644), and one tract of which the subject is of a more general and permanent nature, the best known of all the series: —"Areopagitica:—A Speech for the Liberty of unlicensed Printing, to the Parliament of England," 1644.—The whole series extends thus over a period of somewhat less than twenty years; the earliest, viz. "Of Reformation touching Church Discipline in England, and the causes that hitherto have hindered it," having been published in 1641, the latest, entitled:—"A ready and easy way to establish a free Commonwealth," coming out in March 1660, after the torrent of royalism had set in which was to sweep away the men and the cause to which Milton had devoted himself; this is the boldest and most powerful of all Milton's English pamphlets. It is full of undying republican fervour, of unmitigated hatred and contempt of the Stuart dynasty, but also full of a wailing and mournful earnestness, and a desperate secret sense of a lost cause runs through it.

Milton's hand is also to be clearly traced in the leading articles of a newspaper entitled "Mercurius politicus," which appeared about 1650; some of them may even be wholly of his composition.

To complete the list of his prose writings we have to mention:— "Accedence Commenced Grammar" (1669), a Latin Grammar written in English; "History of Britain," to the conquest (1670); "Of true religion, heresy, schism, toleration, and what best means may be used against the Growth of Popery," his latest utterance on theological topics, published by him the year before his death, 1673. The only matter really discussed in the pages of the tract is the limit of toleration.—Seven years after his death, in 1681, there was published:—

---

[1] 1. Tenure of kings and magistrates. Spring 1649. 2. Observations on Ormond's Articles of Peace, &c. May 1649. 3. Eiconoclastes. October 1649. 4. Letter to a Friend concerning the Rupture of the Commonwealth. 1653. 5. Pro populo Anglicano defensio. 1650. 6. Defensio Secunda. 1654. 7. The present means, and brief delineation of a free Commonwealth. 1659. 8. The Ready and Easy Way. 1660.

[2] 1. Autoris pro se Defensio contra Morum. 1655. 2. Autoris Responsio.

"Mr. John Milton's Character of the Long Parliament, and Assembly of Divines," a passage said to have been omitted from the "History of Britain," and, in 1682, a compilation appeared:—"A brief history of Moscovia."—In 1743, a certain John Nickolls edited:—"The Milton Papers," consisting of letters and addresses to Cromwell and other influential men of the Commonwealth.—

CHAPTER I.

The Style.

BEFORE passing on to the grammatical investigation which forms the main part of our essay, we would ask leave to dwell for a few moments on the peculiarities of Milton's prose style, which necessarily strike us when we read his English pamphlets.

If his great Epic Poem, "Paradise Lost," is to be admired both for the perfection of its form, and for loftiness and power of thought, we find that the latter qualities alone can be attributed to his prose, a manifestation of "left-handed power," as he himself avows.

Indeed we cannot leave a work like "Areopagitica" without an overpowering sense of the majestic grandeur of his genius.— There is, it is true, something impressive in all his composition; there is scholarship in the masterly logic with which he draws out the legions of his arguments into array, and flanks them with the thunder of his eloquence; there is art which surpasses, without repeating, the art of a Demosthenes in constantly bringing before the mind of the reader, in different dress and with different direction of attack, the facts and the conclusions which he wishes him to grasp. But it is in this feature alone that his giant mind excels; in the more delicate branches of his art, his efforts are, as a rule, clumsy.[1]

One of the truest words that Dr. Johnson ever uttered concerning another author, was when he said that "Milton never learned

---

[1] The lecture of Hill, G. F. "Prize Essay" on the Prose Style of John Milton, London, U. Coll., 1885, has inspired many remarks in this chapter.

the art of doing little things with grace; he overlooked the milder excellence of suavity and softness; he was a Lion that had no skill in dandling the Kid."[1] And thus, in spite of the strictly scientific spirit which guided him in the composition of his pamphlets and treatises,[2] the reader will be early to lay a hand of blame on the frequent obscurity of his sentences,—a remarkable peculiarity of his prose style,—on the repeated occurrence of passages in which his constructions are inspired by the Latin syntax, and on the many distinct traces of Euphuism.

Where Milton is obscure to us, he sometimes rivals another prose author of high rank :—Thucydides. There is this difference, however, that the ancient author was obscure for the most part in the extreme pregnancy of every word he used and in its in-timate connection with several different parts of the sentence,[3] while Milton, remarkable as he is for the absence of that "wind" which is so characteristic of Cicero, is most obscure to us where he gives us length of sentences. This is often the case, for Milton hates a writer who makes sentences by the statute, "as if all above three inches long were confiscate." The fact is that he had more to say than he could say. His thoughts rush upon him in a throng that he can at times scarcely order and control. These thoughts natu-rally arrange themselves in relative sentences, and complicated thoughts generate complicated sentences. But beneath all his prose periods the fire of his poetry may be seen gleaming, and ever and anon it breaks through and blazes up supreme; then, the poet bears us through, to the end of the longest sentences, on the wings of the rhythm and harmony of words which we so constantly and easily discover in them, and of which the few fragments quoted below will give ample illustrations.

---

1 Johnson, Samuel. Lives of E. Poets. Milton. Chandos Classics, p. 65.

2 As an example of it we may mention the careful divisions and subdivi-sions in the discussion of punishment. Reason of Church Government. Book II. Chapter 3.

3 Cicero. De orat. II. 13. 56. Omnes dicendi artificio mea sententia facile vicit; qui, ita creber est rerum frequentia, ut verborum prope numerum sententiarum numero consequatur; ita porro verbis est aptus et pressus, ut nescias utrum res oratione an verba sententiis illustrentur.

Naturally it is in the general colouring of his style that we find Milton's poetical nature showing itself most clearly.

Depreciators of his style, and there are not a few, complain that there is a want of eloquence and poetical spirit in his prose works. But, have they read, have they been able to appreciate that noblest piece of English prose ever written:—the introduction to the second book of the Reason of Church Government? Could they display the rare combination of poetry and learning which marks the first chapter of the first book of the same work? Have they a power of analogy equal to that which, when the "dunce prelates" boast that they are the protectors of the Church from schism, breaks out upon them with:—"The winter might as well vaunt itself against the spring:—I destroy all rank and noisome weeds, I keep down all pestilent vapours; yes, and all wholesome herbs, and all fresh dews, by your violent and hidebound frost:—but when the gentle west winds shall open the fruitful bosom of the earth, thus overgirded by your imprisonment, then the flowers put forth and spring, and then the sun shall scatter the mists, and the manuring hand of the tiller shall root up all that burdens the soil without thank to your bondage?"

Is there imagery and metaphor in them like that which runs through every greater work of Milton? Mark the description of Love in "Doctrine and Discipline of Divorce, I. 6":—"Love, if he be not twin born, yet hath a brother wondrous like him, called Anteros: whom while he seeks all about, his chance is to meet with many false and faining Desires, that wander singly up and down in her likeness. By them in their borrowed garb, Love though not wholly blind, as Poets wrong him, yet having but one eye, as being born an Archer aiming, and that eye not the quickest in this region here below, which is not Love's proper sphere, partly out of the simplicity, and credulity which is native to him, often deceived, imbraces and consorts him with these obvious and suborned striplings, as if they were his Mother's own sons, for so he thinks them, while they subtly keep themselves most on his blind side. But after a while, as his manner is, when soaring up into the high Tower of his Apogæum, above the shadow of the earth, he darts out the direct rays of his then most piercing eyesight upon the impostures, and trim disguises that were used with him, and discerns that this is not his genuine brother, as he imagined, he has no longer the power to hold fellowship with such a personal mate.

For straight his arrows loose their golden heads, and shed their purple feathers, his silk'n breades untwine, and slip their knots, and that original and fiery virtue given him by fate, all on a sudden goes out and leaves him undeified and despoiled of all his force: till finding Anteros at last, he kindles and repairs the almost faded ammunition of his deity by the reflection of a coequal and homogeneal fire."—

I think we may safely say that there are passages of greater grandeur in Milton than in any other English prose-writer. I have instanced some, others are the peroration to "Areopagitica," in which we find these wonderful prophetic words:—"Methinks I see in my mind a noble and puissant Nation rousing herself like a strong man after sleep, and shaking her invincible locks:—Methinks I see her as an Eagle muing her mighty youth, and kindling her undazzled eyes at the full midday beam; purging and unscaling her long abused sight at the fountain itself of heavenly radiance, while the whole noise of timorous and flocking birds, with those also that love the twilight, flutter about, amazed at what she means, and in their envious gabble would prognosticate a year of sects and schisms." Read also the peroration to the sixth chapter of the first book, and —most Miltonic of all—the whole conclusion to the second book of the "Reason of Church Government".—

As to the character of Milton's prose works, it is, of course, as a rule highly polemical. But against all complaints of the violence of his attacks on his enemies, Milton can easily and triumphantly defend himself. He most specially pleads his cause in the long and eloquent passage in the introduction to the second Book of the Reason of Church Government, to which I have so frequently referred, in which he declares, with all the truth in the world on his side, that "no man can be justly offended with him that shall endeavour to impart and bestow, without any gain to himself, those sharp but saving words which would be a terror and a torment in him to keep back,"—quite enough vindication of the part he took in the paper war of his day. It was not himself that he was defending, so much as the truth of the cause for which he was fighting, the "evangelic doctrine which opposes the tradition of prelacy." He was indeed forced to this course of action, refusing as he did "to praise a fugitive and cloistered virtue unexercised and unbreathed, that never sallies out and seeks her adversary, but slinks out of the race where that immortal garland is to be run for, not without dust and heat." If he did in the contest sometimes descend to folly, yet, "how hard is it when a man meets with a fool to keep his tongue from folly."—

The coarseness which sometimes shows itself in his humour is as much a characteristic of his age as is the puritanical enthusiasm with which he is filled. He cannot therefore be blamed for what of coarseness we do find in his pages. Nay, rather, he is to be praised for the remarkable absence of it in most of them. The work in which this kind of humour most comes out is the "Apology for Smectymnuus." There is, however, nothing in the slightest degree immoral in it. It makes us laugh,—who could help laughing at the image of the "foot episcopal, with the four toes prelatical, and the great toe Metropolitan" sending up its stench to heaven?

A peculiarity which must strike every one with regard to Milton's humour is this, that when it is not coarse, it is extremely bitter. He seems to have a talent for catching up a mistake on his adversary's part, explaining it to him, and then with great force and emphasis showing him the consequences. Take one example from the "Reason of Church Government":—"That the Prelates have no sure foundation in the Gospel, their own guiltiness does manifest; they would not else run questing up as high as Adam to fetch their original, as it is said one of them lately did in public. To which assertion, had I heard it, because I see they are so insatiable of antiquity, I should gladly have assented, and confessed them yet more ancient:—for Lucifer, before Adam, was the first prelate angel; and both he, as is commonly thought, and our forefather Adam, as we all know, for aspiring above their orders, were miserably degraded." Milton is somewhat fond of establishing a connexion between the hero of his great epic and prelaty, "who sends her haughty prelates from all parts with their forked mitres, the badge of schism, or the stamp of his cloven foot whom they serve." And he treats in the same way the Star-chamber in the last paragraph of "Areopagitica":—"For this authentic Spanish policy of licencing books, if I have said ought, will prove the most unlicenced book itself within a short while; and was the immediate image of a Star-chamber decree to that purpose made in those very times when that court did the rest of those her pious works, for which she is now fallen from the stars with Lucifer." [1]

A prose so powerful, characterised by so striking idiosyncrasies of its writer, in its moral as well as in its purely aesthetical aspect, was the result of a most careful training, as Milton himself explains: —"I must say therefore that after I had from my first years by the ceaseless diligence and care of my father, whom God recompense, been exercised to the tongues, and some sciences, as my age would suffer, by sundry masters and teachers, both at home and at the schools, it was found that whether ought was imposed me by them that had the overlooking, or be taken to of mine own choice in English, or other tongue, prosing or versing, but chiefly this latter, *the style by certain vital signs it had, was likely to live.*" [2]

CHAPTER II.

English Grammar in the time of Milton.

MILTON'S English, as it is exemplified in the prose works on the study of which the following remarks are based,[3] belongs to that period which Sweet in his "New English Grammar" qualifies as

---

[1] Cf. Hill. Prize Essay.
[2] Reason of Church Government. II. Introd.
[3] Our statements are based on the careful reading of:—
   a. Milton's autograph notes in the Bible printed by Rob. Barker, London, 1612. Brit. Mus. Add. MS. 32310;

Early Modern English (Early Mn. E.; Tudor English; English of
Shakespere), and which he approximatively dates from 1500—1650.
That period is characterised by the fact that in it the language
became mainly uninflectional, with only scanty remains of the older
inflections. It is also the period during which the London dialect
became fully predominant, becoming thus the only one used in
writing throughout England.

Uniformity of spelling, however, and generally acknowledged
rules of Grammar did not exist in any way, and thus, that Early
Modern Period is but a period of experiment and comparative
licence, both in the importation and in the formation of new words,
idioms, and grammatical constructions.—But it was chiefly in the
domain of spelling that the decay of Anglo-Saxon (which, as regards
the inflections, had already attained its highest degree), went on
for a considerable space of time, bringing about great irregularity
and licence which may easily be traced down to our days, where it
makes itself felt in the double—and even multiple—spelling of
many words.

And yet it is from this Early Modern Period that grammarians
date the epoch of reorganisation of the language,—a reorganisation
which was due, in great part, to the influence of the Romance

b. the prose passages (fac-similes) found in S. L. Sotheby's "Ramblings
in the Elucidation of the autograph of Milton." London, 1861;

c. "A Common-place book of John Milton reproduced by the autotype
process from the original MS." Edited by A. J. Horwood, under the
direction of the Royal Society of Literature. London, 1876;

d. Milton's pamphlet "Of Prelatical Episcopacy" (12 pages read). London,
1641. 4⁰;

e. his pamphlet "The Reason of Church Government." London, 1641. 4⁰;

f. "Animadversions upon the Remonstrants defence against Smectymnuus." London, 1641 (17 pages read);

g. on a very careful study of "Areopagitica." London, 1644, and ed.
Hales, Clar. Press. 1886;

h. "Of Education." To Master Samuel Hartlib. London, 1644;

i. "The Doctrine and Discipline of Divorce;" Book I. Cap. 1—6.
London, 1645.

k. "Eikonoklastes." London, 1649 (12 pages read).

We have confined ourselves to the study of works written and published
before 1652, for we do not know how far Milton may be made responsible for the
spelling, in the first editions of his pamphlets, after his having lost his sight.—

(French) element, which not only enriched its vocabulary, but also furthered and assisted the development of its whole system. Those grammarians are, in the main, right.

The authority of Chaucer, who was the father, as it were, of correctly written English, had long been prevailing, but it began to be questioned, when the rules of spelling set down and observed by him could no more be recognised universally, because they could not be made to harmonise with the spoken language, whose sounds went on changing with even greater rapidity than before.—The need of a grammar was therefore strongly felt in England, and many an attempt was made to bring about uniformity of spelling and of accidence, and to teach the people correct writing and pronunciation. In the following pages we shall endeavour to complete, as far as possible, what Mr. A. Ellis, in his work on Early English Pronunciation, has been writing summarily on the grammarians of the first half of the seventeenth century, and in subsequent chapters we shall have frequent occasion to refer to the books discussed here.[1]

The Latin schoolbooks used by previous generations were still kept in honour in the Grammar Schools, and it was not till the beginning of the XVIIIth century that reliable books on grammar, methodically arranged for the use of the progressing pupils, came into use in the schools of the people, while Grammar Schools went on following the old line for some time yet.[2]

The old *Hornbook*, with its alphabet, Lord's Prayer and a few lines to spell and read, had been in general use till the XVth century. As late as 1716 Hornbooks were to be bought for two pence.

It had been followed by the *Battledore*, so named because used as a toy by the children, of similar character, but different in form, two pages folding on a third in the centre.—The *Primer* succeeded,

---

[1] Mr. J. A. Ellis, in "On E. E. Pronunciation," London, 1871—1874, discusses the following authors (the dates indicate the year of the publication of their work):—J. Hart, 1569; Bullokar, W[m]; Gill, A.; Butler, Ch.; Mulcaster; Black Letter Book, 1602; Ben Jonson, 1640; Gataker, Tho[s], 1646; Willis, Tho[s], 1651; Wallis, John, 1653—1699; Wilkins, John, 1668; Price, Owen, 1668; Holder, W[m], 1669; Poole, Josua, 1677; Cooper, C., 1685; Miege, Guy, 1688. Cf. Ellis, On Early English Pronunciation, I. 26, 35, 36 et seq., to p. 69.

[2] Cf. The Bookseller. Oct. 3[d] 1871, p. 818. "An article on Schoolbooks."

which was not only a spelling-book, but also a reading-book, hymn-book, and picture-book combined; handy little six-penny books, which can be bought to this day.

In 1568, there appeared a more compendious book:—*"A shorte dictionary for younge Beginners, gathered of good authors, specially Columel, Grapald and Pliny."* Author unknown.[1]

Now this dictionary was followed in 1580 by the first serious attempt at a scientific exposition of English spelling:—*Bullokars Booke at large, for the amendment of orthographie for English Speech.*[2] This curious black spelling-book has a preface:—"Bullokar to his countrie," in which Bullokar tells us:—"I did meane to put it in print above two years past, had I not then understanded by a friende of mine that the like was already handled in print, by Sir Tho' Smith and maister Chester, of whose workes nor the like done by any other I never understood untill then."[3]

In a prologue in 102 verses (14 syllabic iambs), the author sings the praise of language given by God to man and wife, and goes on in the first chapter to discuss the old ABC, and to expound the causes which have led him to amend it.

He begins his "amendment" in the third chapter, discussing many letters, without any method, and introduces abbreviative signs to replace all the letters that are not sounded and which he carefully drops in writing.—He states that 6 letters of the old alphabet are alone perfect:—a, b, d, f, k, x, whereas the English language possesses 37 different sounds, and after having gone so far as to say, in the VIth chapter, that even the other nations will be assisted in their treatment of language by his improvements, he draws up his alphabet:—37 different signs for 37 sounds, which he briefly explains. From the VIIth chapter onward, he gives examples, first

---

[1] I have been unable to find the book.

[2] Bullokar, William, Phonetist, ab. 1520—1590, was engaged in teaching for the best part of his life; he studied agriculture and law. He published:—*Pamphlet for spelling*, 1580; *Aesop's Fables* translated into English from the Latin, 1585; *A Bref Grammar* ("the first that ever was except my grammar at large"), 1586.—The latter is not at the Brit. Museum. The *Booke at Large* has 59 pages, after a prologue and a preface.

[3] The two books here referred to have never been found.

of words,—beginning with "a ballanc'"—and ending with "too hóp,"—*always using double consonants to express shortness of vowel;* the VIIIth chapter contains examples "of paiers of vowels and halfe vowels;" in the IXth chapter follow examples of spelling, dividing words into their syllables; from the XIth chapter to the end, he makes use of his own signs, and repeats in a but slightly more concise form all that has gone before. He ends in the XIIth and XIIIth chapter by giving whole pieces of reading in prose and verse.

The influence of Bullokar's book does not seem to have made itself deeply felt,—it did not go through any more editions. It was followed in 1596 by a most interesting philological work, entitled :—

The English Schoolmaster, teaching all his scholars, of what age so ever, the most easie, short and perfect order of distinct reading, and true writing of our English tongue that hath ever yet been known or published by any. And further also, teacheth a direct course, how any unskillfull person may easily both understand any hard English words, which they shall in the Scriptures, sermons, or els-where hear or read:—and also be made able to use the same aptly themselves; and generally whatsoever is necessary to be known for the English speech:—so that he which hath this Book only, needeth to buy no other to make him fit from his Letters unto the Grammar School, for an Apprentice, or any other his private use, so far as concerneth English. And therefore is made not only for children, though the first Book be meer childish for them, but also for all other, especially for those that are ignorant in the Latine tongue. Devised for thy sake that wantest any part of this skill, by Edward Coote, Master of the Free-School in St. Edmunds Bury. Now the 31 time imprinted. London. Seybourn, for the company of Stationers, 1662.

This 31st edition is the sole now extant at the British Museum, but it appears from what Coote says in the preface that the book had been printed for the first time in 1596; it had been printed 33 times by 1665, and 42 times by 1684. (The second part gives the pronunciation of English words in 1668).

In the opening words, "the schoolmaster his Profession," Coote undertakes "to teach his scholars that they shall never erre in writing the true orthography of any word truly pronounced." The "Profession" (2 pp.) is followed by "the Preface for directions to the reader"

(3 pp.), in which the schoolmaster introduces his method, praising it as giving far more ease and pleasure to the learner, the result of which is far more speed; to bring this about, he has "put no more letters than are of absolute necessity," writing:—templ, tun (= tune), plum (= plume). He addresses himself to the people at large, but chiefly to the less educated classes, "small tradesmen and such like," his object is to enable them to spell correctly, in order that they may not be ashamed of writing a letter to a friend; so he drops all that is not essential, proper names, for instance, the spelling and use of which is so unsettled.—After having exposed his alphabetical table, he begins, on page 1 of the first part, by giving us a list of simple open syllables:—fo, la; on page 2, closed syllables:—fog, lad, and so on through eight chapters, passing from simple words to complicated ones, in sound and spelling, thus:—*ca, cat, caught; gir, girdl.*

In the second part of his book, beginning at page 11, we are taught the division of words into syllables, again by simple lists of words; the rules which those examples are to illustrate are laid down as marginal notes.—Letters not pronounced are discussed in chapter IV; from chapter V onward we have sundry other observations for perfecting the scholar, and we shall have occasion to refer to them below. The last chapter, the VIIIth, contains more spelling examples. In the third part of the work we find a great variety of pieces for reading: a short catechism, prayers, a few chapters taken from the book of proverbs, the psalms taken from the prayer-book, and finally some "arithmetick" and a very interesting list of the most important dates in the history of the world: a first period goes from the birth of Seth, in the year 130 from the Creation of the World, to 1650 date of the Universal Flood; the second period covers from the year 2 after the Universal Flood to the Law given in 858; the third period ends with the birth of Christ; the last period covers from the birth of Christ to the year 500, when the Goths conquered Italy.

From the 58th page to the 77th (to the end of the book), we have a "vocabulary for the unskilful how to spell;" it contains about 1300 words; expressions not likely to be known are explained, thus:—"Apostasie" is "falling away;" "Lapidarie" means "skilful in stones."

That little book must have been very favourably received by those for whom it was compiled, the enormous number of editions it went through in a comparatively short time clearly shows its extraordinary popularity. It was intended to be a practical guide for the non-educated, and the author fully succeeded in making it to be so.

Twenty years seem to have elapsed before John Bullokar [1] felt himself induced to publish his *"English Expositor"*:—*"teaching the interpretation of the hardest words used in our Language, with sundry explications, descriptions and discourses. London. Printed by John Legatt, 1616."* A large number of words had come in to increase the English vocabulary through the channel of French, Italian and Spanish, but their meaning was still unknown to the people at large, and the *Expositor* was doubtless needed. After a dedicatory Epistle to "Lady Jane Vicountesse Mountague," and a few words addressed to the reader, the author gives us a long list of words, nearly all of foreign origin, and endeavours to make their meaning clear to his countrymen. Thus, he explains:—

    Abbreviate = to make short,
                to abridge;

    Ablution   a washing;

    Baptist or washer   St. John the sonne of Zacharias, was so called for that hee first began to baptize or wash men in the river of Jordan to the remission of sinnes.

    Catholike = a greeke word signifying universall or generall.

---

[1] Bullokar, John, ab. 1580—1641, Doctor of physic, residing at Chichester in 1616, was attached to "Ladie Jane Viscountesse Mountague." He wrote his *Expositor* in his youth, "at the request of a worthy gentleman whose love prevailed much with him," and gave it to the world in 1616. The second edition appeared in 1621, the third in 1641, shortly after which he must have died, for a fourth edition, which appeared in 1656, is said "to be newly revised, corrected and, with the addition of above a thousand words, enlarged. By W. S." A fifth edition appeared at Cambridge in 1676 under the editorship of a "lover of the arts." The seventh edition bears the date 1684, a sixth must then have shortly followed the fifth. The eighth and last appeared in London, in 1719, and was prepared by R. Browne, author of "The English School Reform'd."

It is a decided improvement on the *Booke at large* of William Bullokar as regards the uniformity of the spelling, and we shall have occasion to refer to the *Expositor* now and again.

Three years later Milton's master, Alexander Gil, of St. Paul's School, published for the use of the schoolboys who knew Latin, his *Logonomia Anglica, qua gentis sermo facilius addiscitur. Conscripta ab Alexandro Gil, Paulinae Scholae magistro Primario. Londini. Excudit Johannes Beale, 1619.*[1] The dedicatory Epistle to King James I., in Latin, is followed by a preface to the reader, in Latin as well. In that preface Gil tries to sketch the history of the English tongue, praising it as most practical and worthy to become the universal language. He adds a few remarks on the desirability of introducing a new spelling, the spelling in use at his time being most corrupt; he alludes, as Bullokar had done before, to attempts at a reform by Thomas Smith, "ex equestri ordine," by Thomas Mulcaster and by Chester. No mention is made of Coote's Schoolmaster.

The first chapter begins with a definition:—"Logonomia est comprehensio regularum quibus sermo ignotus facilius addisci potest."—The study of a language comprises four parts:—Grammar, Etymology, Syntax, Prosody.—The sounds, the syllables, the rules of spelling are carefully exposed in the seven chapters of the first part.—The second part:—"Etymologia," chapter VIII—XIII, to page 62, treats of derivation, composition, comparison, diminution, then of "Vocum species":—noun, pronoun, verb; "de consignificativis":—article, adverb, conjunction, preposition, interjection.— The "Syntax," chapter XIV—XVIII, treats of adjectives, numbers, substantives and their cases, and of the verbal construction.—The last part, devoted to Prosody, is an illustration of the rules of Poesy, by examples taken from Spenser's "Faery Queene;" a last word "Παραίνεσις" to the reader, containing an honourable mention of

---

[1] Alexander Gill, the Elder, 1565—1635, high-master of St. Paul's School, was born in Lincolnshire ab. 1564—1565. In March 1607—1608 he became high-master of St. Paul's School in succession to R. Mulcaster. He was famous not only as a schoolmaster, but also as a "learned man, a noted Latinist, critic, and divine." He wrote:—1. A treatise concerning the Trinitie of Persons in Unitie of the Deitie. Lond., 1601, 8°, 2ᵈ ed. 1635. 2. Logon. Angl., 1619, 2ᵈ ed. 1621. 3. Sacred Philosophie of the Holy Scripture. Lond., 1635, 8°; with reprint of 1. Cf. R. Stern, "Milton und seine Zeit," I, 31, 42, 80, 206.

Minshaw,—author of the "Ductor ad linguas,"—concludes the work of 150 pages.—Written as it was by a scholar for scholars, this work could not possibly have been of great influence on the language at large, but Milton knew of it, and we shall occasionally have to refer to it.

A very curious book was published in the year 1624, under the title:—*"A perfect survey of the English tongue, taken according to the use and analogie of the Latine, and serveth for the more plaine exposition of the Grammaticall Rules and Precepts, collected by Lillie and for the more certain translation of the English tongue into Latine.*

Together with sundry good demonstrations, by way of sentences in either tongue. Written and collected by John Hewes, Master of Arts.

Principiis cognitis, multo facilius extrema intelligentur. (Cicero pro Cluentio.) London. Printed by Edward All-de for William Garret. 1624."

The main object of the author was to assist students in the translation of "the English tongue into Latine." He starts from the English grammar as basis, he exposes it systematically and clearly, and to every English rule he opposes the Latin rule fitting the case. We have thus practically two grammars in one book; and Hewes' considerations on the English language are often remarkably clear and worthy of our attention. The book seems to have been appreciated; the Bishop of London, to whom it is dedicated, must have taken a deep interest in the endeavours of the author, and another proof of his success are the eight epigrams found between the dedication and the preface, seven in Latin and one in English, written by friends of Hewes, in the author's praise. The preface "to all teachers of the art of Grammar in the Latin tongue" (6 pp.) contains the following words, which we quote in order to justify our mention of the work in this place:—"I have heere made an exact survey of the English tongue, as the same may for the use of all the parts of speech in composition best conduce or accord with the Latines, and so I have made as a posteriori the English tongue for those that are English, the first ground worke to the Latine."

Accordingly, the first part of his work is an exposition of the English tongue, in which he discusses first the parts of speech, their characteristic signs and use (e. g. "*A* and *the* are signes of noune substantive "), "the moodes, the tenses, the generall rules of the syntax of the cases." Cases according to him can only be marked by prepositions, of the Saxon genitive he makes no mention.

Then he goes on to state the Latin rules of concord, and the second part of this grammar does not lie within the range of our discussion.

Near the end, on the 100th page, Hewes speaks of the "difference between the dialect of the Latines and that of the English," and ends with:—"The author his counsell and Exhortation to his beloved Pupils and those of all ages." It is a praise of the art of grammar, "the doore to all good Artes and Institutions;" he fills 16 pages with this encomium, declaring learning to be a necessity for the state. "Learning is a glory to young men, but it draweth a reverence and honour to the Aged . . . , it seemeth of itselfe to adorne and beautifie all Ages and Degrees."

The year 1633 witnessed the publication of *" The English Grammar, or the institution of letters, syllables and words, in the English tongue; whereunto is annexed an index of words like and unlike. By Charles Butler, Magd. Master of Arts. Oxford. Turner, 1633."* [1] This philological work, to which we shall have occasion to refer later on, contains 63 pages of grammar, in which the author discusses the letters, the syllables, the words (noun substantive, noun adjective, pronouns, verbs, adverbs), the words adjunct; finally:—tone and sound, accent and the "points."—Ellis in his *" Early English Pronunciation "* has given a detailed account of the book.

We pass on, then, to a series of publications by a schoolmaster named Hodges, between 1640—1650, the first of which appeared in 1643, under the title:—*"A special help to orthographie:—or, the true*

---

[1] Butler, Charles, philologist, was born at Great Wycomb (probably). On leaving Oxford, in 1587, he received the mastership of the free school at Basingstoke, Hamps., together with the curacy of Skewres which he held for 7 years. He was then for 48 years vicar of Lawrence-Wotton, where he died on the 29th of March 1647. His works are:—1. The Feminine Monarchie, or a Treatise concerning Bees and the due ordering of Bees. 1609, 8°; 2^d ed. 1623; 3^d ed. 1634, was printed in phonetic spelling:—" The Feminin' Monarchi', or the Histori of Bees;"—2. A Latin treatise on Rhetoric, 1629;—3. Συγγένεια, on affinity as a bar to marriage, 1625;—4. English Grammar, 1633; 2^d ed. 1634;—5. The Principles of Music in singing and setting, Lond. 4°, dedicated to Prince Charles, 1636.

*writing of English. Consisting of such words as are alike in sound and unlike
both in their signification and writing:—as also of such words which are so
near alike in sound that they are sometimes taken one for another. Whereunto
are added diverse orthographical observations, very needfull to be known.
Publisht by Richard Hodges, a School Master dwelling in Southwark, at the
Midle-gate within Mountague-close, for the benefit of all such as do affect
True-Writing. London. March 2ᵈ. Printed for Richard Cotes, 1643."*—

In the first 27 pp. we have a series of examples, alphabetically
arranged, illustrating the use of "such words as are alike in sound,
and unlike both in their signification and writing, expresst by different
letters." Forty examples fall under A, for instance:—To *assent* or
agree; an *ascent* or going up; a *sent* or savour.—Let him that hath *a
loud* voyce, be *allow'd* to speak *aloud.*—22 ex. of words beginning
with B, ex.: To *bow* the knee; the *bough* of a tree.—22 ex. of words
beginning with C:—*Cox*, an mans sirname; *cocks* and Hens; *cocketh*
up the hay.—D gives nine examples:—It is not worth a *dollar;* ful
of *dolour* and griefe.—E yields 7 examples, F 18, G 9, H 21, I 3,
J 7, K 3, L 12, M 17, N 3, O 6, P 15, R 30, S 35, T 20, V 4,
W 11, Y 5.—

Then follow "such words which are so neer alike in sound,
as that they are sometimes taken one for another, are also expressed
by different letters, in these examples following." 11 examples are
given of words beginning with A; (ex: *Ask* the carpenter for his *ax*,
whereby he hath done such strange *acts;* the *ant* is a wise crea-
ture; an uncle and an *aunt.)* — 23 examples are given of words
beginning with B; *(bowes* and arrows; *boughs* and branches.) 12
examples of words with C; (his *chaps* are ful of *chops.)* Words beginning with D yield 11 examples, with E 8, with F 12, G 5, H 10,
I 9, K 3, L 8, M 13, N 5, O 4, P 27, R 8, S 28, T 8, U 5, W 12.

Hodges then gives a few "examples of some words wherein
one sound is expresst diverse ways in writing." So:—*se*ated, con-
*ce*ited, *sei*zing, *se*rious, *sce*va, *ce*dar, manas*seh*, Phari*see*, Woolse*y*, *sch*edule,
*cea*sing, and so on.—The important part of the book, however, lies in
the "special observations very needful to bee known, for the help
of true writing," made concerning the use of consonants and vowels;
they will often be referred to in this essay. Strange to say, however,

THE ENGLISH
PRIMRÔSE:

Far furpaſſiñg âl others of this kinde, that ever
grêw in any Engliſh garden : bŷ the ful
fight whêreof, there wil ma-
nifeſtly appêar,

The Eaſieſt and Speedieſt-way, bôth for the
trúe ſpelliñg and rêadiñg of Engliſh, as
alſô for the Trúe-writiñg thereof :
that ever was publickly
known tô this day.

Planted (with nô ſmâl pains) bŷ Richard
Hodges, a School-maſter, dwelliñg in Southwark, at the midle-gâte within Moun-
taguе-clôſe : for the exceediñg grêat
benefit, bôth of his ôwn Coun-
trêy-men and Strangers.

Approved âlſô bŷ the Learned, and publiſht
bŷ Âuthority.

If the trumpet give an uncertain ſound, whô
ſhâl prepâre himſelf tô the battel? 1 Cor. 14. 8

LONDON
Printed for Richard Cotes. 1644.

Fac-simile of the title page of Hodges' *English Primrose* (p. 17).

Hodges after having stated the case, and discussed the convenience, or the inconvenience, of the spelling in use, does not venture to sum up in a definite rule; he always humbly says:—"I leave these things to the consideration of the learned."—He was not writing for the learned, then, as it appears still more clearly from the publication of his next little book (120 pp.), whose title page is interesting enough to be reproduced here.[1]

In his preface to the reader, he declares in the first place that every man's object ought to be to know God; in order to know God we must be able to read the Bible; therefore our great aim in life is to be the gaining of sacred knowledge. But this is hard and difficult for master and pupil, and the fault does not alway lie with the pupil when he is punished, "but in the uncertain, and perplext and intricate expressing of our Tongue, by letters wrong named; and by their various sounds and forces attributed to them;" so he will endeavour to show "how the inconvenience and uncertaintie in our expressing the English Language may be remedied without infringing of custom;" he will do this by introducing marks of distinction for the consonants.—His own spelling however is, in the preface, very unsettled.

Hodges adds to it a short poem of 26 ten syllabled lines, "The authours invitation to al such as are ignorant, to gain the knowledge of reading the Holy Scriptures, by means of his book."

There follows a "New Hornbook," being an exposition of the letters and sounds, with their names. 13 vowels and diphthongs and 29 consonants are distinguished, and signs introduced to distinguish the consonants among themselves; _e_ mute is to be denoted by e̲, mod. ū, ō are written û, ô, mod. ä and ë   ä, ë. Unfortunately the discussion and explanation of vowels long and short, of diphthongs and consonants, is so confuse that we must not be astonished if the author himself, when he attempts to use his own modified alphabet, shows great uncertainty and clumsiness. I have failed to discover an explanation of the meaning of the signs —, ⌒, ‿, ⊂ used with consonants.

---

[1] A photograph of the title page was taken for me by Mr. James Hyatt, 47, Great Russell-st., London, W.C. The book is in the Brit. Museum.

Pages of spelling examples follow, of syllables with two letters;
then come lists of words illustrating:— 1) syllables which can be used
both at the beginning and at the end of a word; 2) such syllables
as can only be used at the end; 3) such syllables as can only be
used at the beginning of words. The same course is adopted to
exemplify the use of syllables with *three* letters, then with *four* letters;
and finally 27 pages of more complicated syllables, and words to be
spelt. Various pieces follow, as reading exercises, and are, of course,
all taken from the Holy Scripture. Finally we find in the *"Primrose"*
"Certain brief rules for the true spelling of any English word, or the
dividing of it into syllables;" the syllable is defined, we are shown
how to divide a word into syllables. An example of those rules
may be quoted:—"1st. If two vowels come together both fully pro-
nounc't and no diphthong, you must put the first of these to the
syllable aforegoing and the latter of them to the syllable following,
as in cre-ate, cre-a-ted. 2nd. Double consonants are to be divided:—
ad-der, bet-ter."

The rules of punctuation are likewise exemplified. The numbers,
cardinal and ordinal ("expressing the order of any thing"), are next
discussed, to them are added a table of numeration and one of
multiplication, and the book closes with:—"An answer to give satis-
faction to al such who think that this new way of teaching wil dis-
courage learners, because there are more letters to bee learned than
were before." On the contrary, says Hodges, "it is a cause of exceeding great encouragement, because they shal now learn letters with
greater certaintie than ever;" hitherto people used to express all the
different sounds of one vowel ·by the same sign, whereas now, it
will be easier for them to write and read, since a difference is to be
made in the representation of the various sounds of *o* in modest,
money, moving, motion, mother; so also between the various sounds
of *u* in:—bustle, bugle, bushes, bury, busy; one sees at once that *o*
in the following words is to be sounded in seven different ways:—

tongs, tongues, note, nought, womb, woman, women.—The
author leaves us now, after having expressed his readiness to accept
any proposals or suggestions that might improve his system. The
innovation, then, would consist in the introduction of the following

signs: ᴗ, ᴖ, —, ᨀ, above and below the letters of the alphabet,
ᴄ ᴐ below, and ᴧ above them.

— upon or under a vowel or a consonant denotes that it is not
to be sounded:—sig̅ht. ᴧ upon vowels denotes length, âlsô, kînde,
bŷ, nôte, bûgle. ᴖ, below consonants and vowels, seems to denote
their being open, mọther, iṇ. ᴗ, above and below consonants and
vowels, would then denote their being closed, mọney, dwelliṇg̅.

ᨀ gives to *e* the sound ē in mod. *"Peter"* and to *a* the sound
ā, as in mod. *"lake;"* so gäte, ëạsiest, grëat, prëpäre; but then how
are we to account for ᨀ in thëre? as to ᴐ and ᴄ, I fail to discover
their meaning; ᴄ never occurs except under *h* in *th*, under *f* in oꞔ.—
Hodges himself makes *very* sparing use indeed of these signs in his
book, and never, as said above, condescends to give us a clear explanation of their meaning; the discussion of this proposed reform
might form the subject of another essay.

That curious little book, the *"Primrose,"* did not prove successful; the author's method had been attacked, and his last words leave
us under the impression that he himself was not quite satisfied with
it, for it was not practical in any way. But Hodges did not rest
until he had made another attempt to settle the question of spelling
and grammar in a new treatise, entitled:—*"The Plainest Directions for
the true Writing of English, that ever was hitherto publisht:—Especially of
such words whose sounds are altogether alike, and their signification altogether
unlike:—and of such whose sounds are so neer alike that they are often times
taken one for another. Whereunto are added divers useful tables. Invented
by Richard Hodges, a wel-wisher to learning. London. Printed by
Wm Dugard for Tho^t Euster at the Gun in Ivie Lane. June 29. 1649."* *(66pp.)*

This is simply a second edition of the author's "Special Help
to Orthographie, &c.," slightly augmented and revised. He begins
by giving under A "44 words (instead of 40) as are altogether alike
in sound, and unlike both in their signification and writing, most
plainly exprest by different letters in examples" such as this:—"Hee
did assent thereunto, at the ascent of the Hil, and hee smelt there
such a sent or savor, that was verie offensive."—One difference is
this, that Hodges now gives no more the mere words, but forms

short sentences, so under C, we find:—"Mr. Cox wil kil his cocks and hens before he cocketh up his hay."

The "special observations, very needful to bee known, for the help of true writing" follow on page 40, and they turn out to be the same as in the "Special Help," except in one or two passages; the passage in which "*g*" is discussed, as in "*judgment,*" where he had said, "Special Help," p. 18, "but as for things of this kinde, I have spoken at large in another work, which I intend yer long to publish,"—is now altered to:—"but as for things of this kinde, and how they may be remedied, I refer thee (reader) to another Book that is call'd:—The English Primrose, which is sold by John Hancock in Cornhill, at the entrance into Popeshead-Alley," p. 42.

In concluding his observations he says:—"If thou desirest to know further, I refer thee to another Book which will shortly com forth which is cal'd:—The Plainest Way to true spelling, True Reading, and True Writing of English;" this book has not been found, but it shows us how actively Hodges tried to be of some help to his countrymen, because he felt most acutely that something had to be done in order to bring the English spelling on a firm basis. This book, like the "*Primrose,*" closes with some tables of numeration, and Hodges ends with an advertisement concerning his "*Enchiridion Arithmeticon, or a manual of Millions, wherein people (after the plainest manner) may both suddenly and truly see their accounts ready cast up.*"

On the whole, this book is far more carefully written than "A Special Help." The list of "words like and unlike" are in a better alphabetical order; so Ba is followed by Be, Bo, Bl, Br . . . . ; the author is endeavouring to arrive at uniformity of spelling; he drops with greater regularity mute final *e* in *som, to observ;* in *to do, I leav, don;* he now spells *written,* throughout, instead of *writen,* and so on.

We may be inclined to ask why such an industrious worker as Hodges has left so few traces in the history of English philology. The answer is close at hand:—Hodges was not a scholar in the true sense of the word; he did not know that true scholarship, true learning does not lie in extension of knowledge, but in the depth of it. His works on spelling and grammar lack depth of study, and the consequence of it is great uncertainty. And he himself failed to possess that power of concentration which is the first condition of scientific research; he can turn to any occupation:—having written on grammar and spelling, and worked out a new system—but what a system!—he sets to work on a practical guide for keeping accounts! He is confuse in his explanations, and, in his endeavours to be practical, he sadly failed.

In this very superficial survey of English grammar in Milton's time, we have arrived at the end of the first half of the XVIIth century. The works of Milton of which we made a special study with a view to the writing of this essay, all fall within that period, and we might take the year 1650 as the limit of this account of the grammarians, but for completeness' sake, we would just mention the few grammatical works which appeared during the latter half of the XVIIth century, to which reference has to be made more than once in the course of our remarks. Keeping them in chronological order, we find that the next treatise appeared in 1668, under the title:— *"English Orthographie; or the art of right spelling, reading, pronouncing and writing all sorts of English words, wherein such as one can possibly mistake, are digested in an Alphabetical order, under their several short yet plain rules, &c. . . . , printed at Oxford, for Henry Hall, published in London by Francis Titon."* This book, without any author's name, was probably compiled by Messrs. Price and Owen, Oxford students, to whom, at the end of the book, in an advertisement, some more educational works are ascribed.—The instructions are in question and answer, and the book, like its successors, contains not only spelling lessons, but a little of everything.

According to the "Bookseller," there was published in 1677 *"A new spelling Book of Reading and spelling English made Easie, by Thomas Lye. Philanglus. London."* [1]

---

[1] Lye, Lee, or Leigh, Thos, 1621—1684, a non conformist minister, was headmaster of Bury-St. Edmund school for a short time, in 1647. He was very popular as an instructor of children, and was singularly successful in catechising them. He probably kept a school at his house in Clapham. The "New Spelling book" went through a second edition in 1677. Lye also published "The child's delight," about 1674.

The mode in which spelling is taught in this curious little volume, will be seen by a single example:—*Ge-ge-ntlman, the that gentle is; who can rule his mad passions is the "gentlman".*—This may be one and the same with *"Lye's Spelling Book,"* mentioned by the Westminster Review, 1871, page 566, bearing the title *"A new spelling Book:—or Reading and spelling English made easie. Wherein âll the words of our English Bible are set down in an Alphabetical order and divided into their distinct Syllables. Together with the Grounds of the English Tongue laid in Pictures, Words and Verse, wherein are couched many Moral Precepts.—By the help where of (with Gods Blessing) Little children and others of ordinary capacities may in a few months be enabled exactly to read and spell the whole Bible. The fourth Edition. By Thos Lye. Philanglus. London. Printed for Thos Parkhurst, at the Bible and three Crowns, in Cheapside, near mercers chappel, 16 . . ."* (about 1680). The paper failed to take the impression of the last two figures. We have not been able to find these two books, and cannot therefore enter into a more detailed discussion of their character and merits, the last mentioned of the two, might perhaps be the fourth edition of the first, published in 1677. The information found in the "Westminster Review" and in the "Bookseller" is very scanty.

The Westminster Review, 1871, page 566, mentions a third book of Lye's:—*"The Child's Delight, together with an English Grammar, 1684,"* which is not to be found in the British Museum Library. Rich information concerning the rules of spelling in general use in England during the XVIIth century, may be found in the grammar which a Frenchman compiled for the use of his countrymen who might desire to become acquainted with the English language:— *"Nouvelle Méthode pour apprendre l'Anglois, avec une nomenclature françoise et angloise, un recueil d'expressions familières et de dialogues familiers et choisis. Par le Sieur Guy Miege. A Londres. For Thomas Bassett at the George near St. Dunstan's Church in Fleet-street. 1685."* [1]

[1] Miege, Guy, 1644—1718, miscellaneous writer, was a native of Lausanne. He studied philosophy in Switzerland, and left Lausanne in 1661. He arrived in London in March of the same year, became a member of the household of the Earl of Elgin, then undersecretary to the Earl of Carlisle, and was sent as an ambassador to Russia, Sweden, Denmark. During his travels in France, in 1669,

Miege openly confesses, p. 28:—"Il y a ceci d'incommode dans l'orthographe Angloise, que pour exprimer par écrit neuf ou dix sons, on s'y sert de plus de soixante manières différentes;" and further, p. 29:—"La source de ces défauts: c'est qu'en plusieurs mots on a retenu l'ancienne ortographe, en changeant la prononciation; en d'autres mots, tout au contraire, on a changé l'ortographe, et retenu la prononciation. . . . On n'a pas inventé assez de figures ou de lettres, pour exprimer tous les sons distinctement."—Speaking of the need of a reformed, simplified spelling,—"purger l'ortographe,"—he says:—"C'est le souhait de bien des gens d'esprit parmi les Anglois. Mais on y trouve tant d'obstacles et l'on y fait si peu de progrès, que je ne saurais me promettre aucune grande réformation de ce côté-là."

In the first part of his book, from page 7—35, he discusses the "Lettres et les syllabes." The second part (pp. 36—117) treats of the Words and Sentences.

The second half of the book contains:—1) "Nouvelle Nomenclature françoise et angloise, et un recueil d'expressions familières." We have there a vocabulary of 43 pages, in which we can learn to name:—the parts of the human body, the world, Man, the parts of a house, &c., the different kinds of carriages used in travelling, the kinds of murder, and the names of the different kinds of torture, as well as the vocabulary connected with an execution; the names of various vices, a vocabulary of names connected with war, an army, weapons, the earth, the fire, the water,—and natural history in general. 2) "Dialogues familiers pour demander ses nécessités," in which we are taught to ask the way, to inquire for lodgings, and to carry on conversations at table and so on. 3) "Dialogues choisis sur divers sujets."—England, London and the English are

---

he prepares his "Relation of the three Embassies," published in English, French and German.—From 1678 onward he seems to have been occupied with teaching French and Geography, in London. His geographical works on England and Great Britain were also translated into French and German. ("The New State of England." Lond. 1691; 6th ed. in 1706. "The Present State of Great Britain." Lond. 1707; 11th ed. in 1748.) He compiled numerous works on French Grammar, Dictionaries, English and French, and translated several works into French. The complete list of his works will be found in the "Dictionary of English National Biography."

discussed.—This very practical little book, with such a copious amount of varied information, was certainly much in favour with the French; for us it is of great value, because we find in it many explanations of English forms which we cannot find elsewhere, and Ellis in his "E. E. Pronunciation" has not failed to give it due consideration.

The various attempts at a "Grammar" which we have briefly reviewed, proved however useless. The attention of the scholars who might have occupied themselves with the science of language was quite absorbed by Latin, still the universal language in which the governments of the nations, as well as the learned and the cultured in every country, carried on their intercourse.—The study and the perfect knowledge of Latin was then the end of culture and education, consequently the demand for Latin grammars was much larger than the demand for an English grammar,—Milton himself wrote one for his pupils.—But the book which ruled over England for a long time, was Wm Lilye's ("The Grammarian," ab. 1466—1523) *"Royal Grammar,"* which was originally written in Latin, but translated for the first time into English in 1641, under the title:—*"An English Grammar:—or a plain Exposition of Lilie's Grammar in English, with Easie and profitable Rules for parsing and making Latine, &c., &c., by R. R. Master of Arts. London, 1641. (183 pp.)* This is throughout a work referring to Latin.—The next English edition appeared in 1685. *"The Royal Grammar compiled formerly by Mr. Wm Lilly, now modestly endeavoured to be rendered plain and obvious to the capacity of youth, by a supplement of things defective and alteration of things amiss, together with a poetical Index by R. C. London, 1685."* And nine years later there appeared:—*" The Royal Grammar Reformed into a more easie Method for the Better Understanding of the English and the more speedy attainment of the Latin Tongue. London. March 6. 1694." (164 pp.)*

From these attempts we see that the spelling of Early Mn. E. aimed at being as phonetic as possible; it was so in intention at least, and we are able to trace distinctly in Milton's writings a strong tendency to uniformity, in the spelling as well as in the accidence. The great care he bestowed on them did not fail to produce a lasting and beneficial influence on the Grammar of the English tongue.

A comparative study of the Prose writers of the first half of the XVIIth century might alone lead to certain conclusions as to the real state of Grammar at that time; this does not lie within our power now, though, of course, reference has been made in this essay to Bacon (1561—1626), Sir Tho[s] Herbert, Jeremy Taylor (1613—1667), Hobbes (1588—1679), Sir Tho[s] Browne (1605—1682).[1] But the most reliable authority is doubtless Milton, who was, as we know, a most accurate and conscientious writer. How could a man be careless in his writings, who, throughout his life, was of a sometimes pedantic accuracy and punctiliousness, both in what we may call the mere details of life—outward life—, in matters connected with dress, bodily care, dwelling and division of time, &c., and in what we consider to be the highest aims of life:— the training of mind and heart, the developing of the nobler faculties and powers, emotional as well as physical?— How could a man fail to be accurate and conscientious himself, who was called upon to teach the young a conscientious and accurate discharge of their duties? For Milton was sometime engaged in the teaching of boys,

---

[1] For the purpose of comparing, we have carefully gone through the following works:—

    a. "The first of the twoo Bookes of Francis Bacon. Of the proficience and advancement of Learning, divine and humane. To the king. At London, Printed for Henrie Tomes, and are to be sould at his shop at Graies Inne Gate in Holborne, 1605." 4⁰. Read:—12 pages.

    b. "A Relation of some yeares Travaile begunne Anno 1626 into Afrique, &c. By T. H(erbert). Esquier. London. 1634." Read:—"A late tragicall history of the Georgians, Christians;" p. 72.

    c.   α. "A discourse concerning prayer extempore or By pretence of the spirit," by J. Taylor. 1646. 4⁰. Read 6 pp.

        β. "A discourse of the Liberty of Prophesying." By Jer. Taylor. 1647. Read 6 pp.

    d. "Humane Nature, or the fundamental Elements of Policy." By Tho[s] Hobbes. 1650. Read 1 chapter, the dedicatory epistle, " to the Reader."

    e. " Hydriotaphia. Urne-buriall." By Tho[s] Browne. 1658. Read the dedication, a letter to Gillingham, 1 chapter.

    f. The extracts from the prose works of Bacon, Taylor, Hobbes and Browne, contained in Arthur Galton's "English Prose, from Maundeville to Thackeray." Camelot Series. London, 1888.

and we know him to have thrown into his lessons the same energy which he carried into everything else. In his eagerness to find a place for everything that could be learnt, there could have been but few hours in the day which were not invaded by careful teaching.[1] There is yet another reason why we should look upon him as an authority in matters of grammar and language:—we know that he did occupy himself with the science of grammar properly so-called; he wrote, as we have seen above, a Latin Grammar for English boys: — "Accedence Commenc't Grammar." — Lastly the mere reading of his prose works clearly shows us that he did care for the manner and form in which his works were brought before the public. We may be convinced that he did not allow a book of his to come out of the press, without having previously carefully corrected the proof-sheets, taking great pains to write as clearly as possible. He appreciated highly a well-written and well-printed book; he says, for instance, in Areop.:—"To be enjoyned the reading of a book at all times, and in a hand scars legible, whereof three pages would not down at any time in the fairest Print, is an imposition which I cannot beleeve how he that values time and his own studies, or is but of a sensible nostrill, should be able to endure."[2]

Indeed there is more uniformity and a greater accuracy to be noticed in his writings than in those of his contemporaries, as well as a tendency to bring his spelling into agreement with the actual pronunciation, in spite of the difficulties with which this was connected, for, as Ellis says (IV, p. 1000), "in this XVIIth century the pronunciation of English altered rapidly, and many words were sounded in a style which, owing to the influence of our orthoepists of the XVIIIth and XIXth centuries, is now generally condemned, although well-known among the less educated classes."

---

[1] Cf. Pattison, "Milton," p. 45. "Edward Phillips, his nephew, held his uncle's memory in great veneration, but when he comes to describe the education he received at his uncle's hands, the only characteristic on which he dwells is that of quantity." Milton supplements this account for us by his written theory: — "Tractate of Education, to Master Samuel Hartlib."—

[2] Areopagitica. Ed. Hales; p. 28, l. 33.

CHAPTER III.

On Spelling.

In the remarks that follow we have confined ourselves to a statement of the most striking orthographical peculiarities found in Milton's prose. He evidently knew of the attempts made to introduce a universally recognised phonetic spelling by John Hart, 1569, Gill, Bullokar, Butler and Hodges,[1] but he does not seem to have held their authority in very high consideration; nay, rather, he was his own authority.

One of the peculiarities which, from the very first, attracts our attention when we read him, is the treatment of weak vowels, chiefly of

A. Weak e.

Weak was generally dropped in Early Mn. E., always when final and inflectional.

1. "At the same time," says Sweet,[2] "double consonants between vowels were shortened, as in M. E. *shilling, fuller, sittinge.* But, as the doubling served to show that the preceding vowel was short, the M. E. spellings were retained, and the doubling was extended to words which in M. E. had a single consonant, as in *penny, herring, copper,* M. E. *peni, hering, coper.* Final *e,* being now silent, was often omitted in writing, so that such words as M. E. *belle* were written *bell* with a final double consonant, which led to a frequent doubling of final M. E. consonants to show shortness of the preceding vowel, as in *all, glass, small,* M. E. *al, glas, smal.*"

---

[1] The earliest attempt at phonetic spelling was the one made by Orrmin, in the XIIth or XIIIth century. Cf. Ellis. E. E. Pron. II, 606.

[2] Sweet. A New English Grammar. Oxford, Clar. Press. 1892. Cf. p. 267.

And Milton accordingly writes:—Ram.,[1] p. 37, 39, 41, to submitt, battell, arrivall, the evills; C. P. B. 111, to forbidd, revells; 181, to incurre; 220, the devill; 221 and 243, the warrs (6 times); Bi.: Christmass; Col.: to permitt, to deferr, to sett down, to stirr; subst. prooffs; Areop. to conferr, to forbidd, to ridd; subst. battell, chappel, libell, sentinell, triall, vassalls, materialls, mineralls, perusall; divell=devil; Anim. 3, stopps; 8, evill; Eikon. 3, subst., warr (4 times); verbs, to deterr, mett, he preferrs; 5, fitt to be abus'd.

Milton also resorted to this means of showing shortness of vowel by doubling consonants in the body of a word, as in:—Ram. 39, the citty (5 times), comming; 40, citty (4 times); C. P. B. 179, comminge (221 and 244). This explains also the spelling of:—a summe, C. P. B. (twice); and of:—forraine, ibid. p. 244; chappell, citty, ghittarrs, forrein, (the latter word being also spelt:—*forein, foreine,* —we never find it spelt *foreign,*—and in fact there should be no *g* in *foreign,* any more than in *sovereign,*—cf. French *forain,* Lat. *foraneus.* So Bacon:—*forrainers, forraine,* whereas Hobbes has:—*forraign*).— Yet we find in Doct. and Disc. of Divorce:—Permited, canot, comits, refer'd; but:—I referre, maries and marries.

This rule was also observed by the best authors of Milton's time. Bacon, for instance, writes (Essay of the true greatnesse of Kingdomes, &c. Cam. Ser.):—Brittaine, citty, sonne, sunne, stemme; he commeth, to mannage, to sett; (Character of Henry VII. Cam. Ser.) arcenalls, counsells, scumme, spialls, intollerable, limitted; (Adv. of L.) evill, parcell, uppon. Where the pronunciation of the preceding vowel was lengthened, the consonant was not doubled:— (Adv. of L.), the fal, I shal, to swel; but also to swell, fill; Herbert (Hist. of G.), requitall, sequell; but:—the two generals; Hobbes (Disso-

[1] The following abbreviations will be used:—Ram.=Ramblings; C. P. B.=Common Place Book; Bi.=Milton Bible; Col.=Colasterion; Areop.=Areopagitica; Eikon.=Eikonoklastes; Prel. Episc.=Of Prelatical Episcopacy; R. of C. G.=Reason of Church Governm.; Anim.=Animadversions; L. to H.=Of Education, letter to Hartlib; Doct. and Disc. of Div.=Doctrine and Discipline of Divorce; Cam. Ser.=Camelot Series; Adv. of L.=Advancement of Learning; Hist. of G.=History of Georgia; Hu. Nat.=Human Nature; α=A disc. concerning prayer; β=A disc. of the Lib. of Prophesying; U. B.=Urne Burial; O. E.=Old English; M. E.=Middle English; Mn. E.= Modern English; E. Mn. E.=Early modern English.

lution of a Commonwealth, Cam. Ser.):—dammage, scabbs, manny; but:—setled, battel; (the ending *el* in battel must have sounded long, for we find the same word spelt:—*battaile,* ˙pl. battailes, throughout in Bacon); (Hu. Nat.), we call and we cal; subst. the ecchoes; Browne (Rel. Medici, Cam. Ser.):—buriall, devill, dogg(e), pitty, starr(e), the fuell, interrment (6 times), (interment); but funerals, a parcel; Jeremy Taylor (A Sermon on the anniv. of Gunpowder Treason. Cam. Ser.), perill; (α), modell, quarrell, councell; (β), vessell; but:—the sum, he cals.

Thus the doubling of a final consonant may be regarded as resulting from the dropping of weak final *e*.

2. "But this doubling was not carried out uniformly. So, also, as the dropping of final *e* in such words as *hate, hope,*—M. E. *haten, hopien,*—would have led to confusion with such words as *hat, hop,* final *e* was kept in them, and at last came to be regarded as a mark of the length of the preceding vowel; accordingly it was added to many words which had no final *e* in M. E., as in *wine, stone, foe*— M. E. *win, stón, fó.*" [1]—With regard to this *e,* we find in Richard Mulcaster's "*Elementarie,*" 1582, the following indications:—" Whensoever *e* is the last and soundeth not, it either qualifieth som letter going before, or it is mere silent, and yet in neither kinde increaseth it the number of syllabs.—I call that *e qualifying,* whose absence or presence, somtime altereth the vowel, somtime the consonant going next before it. It altereth the sound (length) of all the vowels even quite thorough one or more consonants, as:—*máde, stéme, kínde, strípe,* sound sharp with the qualifying *e* in their end, wheras *màd, stèm, frìnd, strìp* sound flat without the same *e.*" [2]

In his discussion of *i, ie* Mulcaster also says:—"If it (*i*) end the last syllab, with one or mo consonants after it, it is shrill (long), when the qualifying *e* followeth" (a sign of length), "and if it be shrill (long) the qualifying *e* must follow, as:—*repíne, unwise, minde, kinde, físte.* If it be flat and quick the qualifying *e* must not follow as:—*inactiv, behind, mist, fist.*" [3]

---

[1] Sweet. N. E. Gr. p. 267.
[2] Cf. Ellis. E. E. Pr. III. 910.
[3] Cf. Ellis. Op. cit. III. 913.

This fully corroborates our remarks on weak final *e*. It explains such spelling as:—imagin, masculin, feminin.

Gill, Logon. Angl. Cap. II. "De literarum compositione" (p. 3 — 5), discusses this *e* and says:--"Syllabae autem productio, inter scribendum dignoscitur dupliciter: Primo, *e* aphono in fine dictionis post consonantem non duplicatam addito: ut, in *dame,* domina, voce monosyllabe; nam *dam* sine *e* aut *damme* cum *e,* post consonam duplicatam est bestiae cujuvis mater. *Grin, greene, bucke, booke.* Et licet in his longis, *e* finalis sepius redundet: Scribimus enim: *seat* aut *seate; meat* aut *meate."*

Butler discusses *e quiescent* in chapter I, § 3, p. 10, of his "Grammar." Having distinguished *e sonant* from *e quiescent,* he goes on to say:—*"E quiescent* is that which, being placed in the ending of a word, is not sounded at all, but only signifieth the former vowel to be pronounced; as in *dame, made,* which otherwise would be short as *dam, mad.*—The absence of it is a sufficient sign of a short:—as in *bile* and *bil, hile* and *hil, bake* and *bak.* So that the *"dubbling"* of a consonant with the adding of *e* (as the manner is) is superfluous, as in *bille, backe, hille, wadde."*

He himself drops everywhere an *e* which is not sounded, and replaces it by an apostrophe; so:—*on', mo'.*—In the pages 12 and 13, he discusses the long vowels, *a, e, o, u, y,* and says that all of them are produced by *"quiescent e."* Ben Johnson (Grammar) explains and alters the passage, saying that it "serves as an accent to produce the vowell preceding."

On page 17 of Hodges' book,[1] we find "some special observations very needful to bee known, for the help of true writing," in which he disapproves of the use of double consonants "with the adding of *e,* so we are not to spel:— *bedde, rodde, budde,* but *bed, rod, bud;* so also *al, bal, wal;* the only exceptions are *ff* and *ss:*—*chaffe, brasse,* (§ 2). Double consonants in the middle of a word are to be avoided, and we are to spel:—*medle, sadle."*

As to weak *e* (§ 4), Hodges says:—"whensoever *e* cometh in the end of any English word whatsoever, except the article *the,*

---

[1] "A special help to orthographie."

it hath no use for sound of it self; and therefore might be altogether left out, if wee had long vowels to express our words
withal; but forasmuch as this is wanting, we are inforc't to make
use of *e* in the end of a word, to shewe thereby, the vowel going
before to bee long. *Vale, male, mane, mare. Val, mal, man, mar.—
Wine, wile—win, wil."* No such sign of length is wanted in words
like *feed, fool, pail,* where we know at once that the vowel-sound is
long. Where misunderstandings might arise, however, *e* is to be
used; thus he says:—"*ea* is short as in these words:—*head, read, stead,
ready, steady;* it is therefore very meet to put an *e* in the end of some
such words, as in *reade,* the present tense, to distinguish it from the
short sound of *read,* the preterimperfect tense." No *e* is needed in
words like *harm, learn, part, hand,* and he goes so far as to wish it
to be dropped in words like *"templ, peopl, giv, liv,"* and in this point
he agrees with Coote, who in his *Schoolmaster* ("Preface for directions
to the reader") says:—"I have put no more letters than are of
absolute necessity," and who consequently spells:—*"templ, tun*
(tune), *plum* (plume)." [1]

Clearly, then, that *e* we so often find at the end of verbs, substantives, adjectives, far from being inflectional, is a mere phonetic
sign of the length of the preceding vowel. We shall have more
than one occasion of giving examples of it.

But these rules were not observed uniformly by the writers of
the time. Milton's spelling varies also; he writes:—Ram. 39, the
house; 40, heavn; receavs; adj. 39, divin justice; verb, 37, to
determin; adv. wher; C. P. B. 183, the cours; 191, the sleevs;
220, divers; 221, shamlesse; 74, therfor; verb: 183, to chok;
Col. to deceav, to deserv, to dissolv, to leav, to perceav, to preserv,
to receav; Doct. and Disc. of Div., to bereav. These explanations
will go a long way towards enabling us to understand the various
cases of weak final *e* discussed in the course of this paper.

3. That the suffix *ate,* of Romance origin, had already been
shortened in English, may be concluded from the fact that we find it
spelt *at* throughout in Milton. C. P. B. 111, obstinat; 185, ingratfull;
221, a continuat poller. Areop. to extirpat, extirpats, to creat, to

---

[1] Cf. Ellis. Op. cit. IV. 1018.

captivat, to participat, to regulat, to separat, to tolerat; adjectives:—
compassionat, consummat, elaborat, frustrat, moderat, obdurat,
obstinat, privat; but:—an illiterate law; subst:—Julian the Apostat,
the magistrat, pl. magistrats, the palat (and once palate), the prelat,
pl. prelats, the tractat, pl. tractats, the senat.—Had the *a* not been
short, as it is in present English, we should no doubt meet a "qualifying" *e* at the end of the word.

4. Weak final *e* was dropped in the word:—cours, fr. course and
cours; in:—to imagin, Masculin, Feminin; it was likewise dropped
regularly after the words:—meer, theam, heer; in the "Letter to
Hartlib," we notice however:—heer, and here (once), theams, meer
and mere, meere.—It is regularly dropped in Areop.:—don, els,
fals, som; but we find:—extreame, encrease; again:—divers, ornate
Rhetorick and determinat sentences. We shall see, then, that Milton
tried to follow, in the main, the rule of *qualifying e,* though in many
cases inaccuracy and uncertainty prevailed.

In the latter half of the century this *e* had come quite out of
use:—"Ce qu'on a fait de plus important dans ce siècle," says
Miège in his introduction, "c'est d'avoir retranché *e* final et muet:—
go, no, so; child, mind; blindness, kingdom;"—and he adds:—"pour ne
pas multiplier les choses sans nécessité, on ne répète plus les con-
sonnes:—*warr, starr; firr, stirr; fitt, bigg."*

5. Very striking too is the omission of mute *e* in the words
themselves; this elision was denoted by an apostrophe, yet not
as a general rule. [1]

Mute *e* is always omitted in the Preterite and Past Participle
ending *ed* of those weak verbs which do not end in *d* or *t.* Ramb. 39,
beseig'd, drownd; 40, humbl'd; 37, immur'd, depos'd, forewarn'd,
lov'd, murder'd, martyr'd, promis'd, reproov'd, stirr'd (twice); 58,
caus'd, murder'd, poyson'd, reveng'd.—C. P. B. 220, spar'd; 243,
hinderd.— Eikon. 5, abus'd, cavill'd, fear'd.—Areop. alter'd, alleg'd,
allow'd, approv'd, ascrib'd, consider'd, convey'd, cry'd, deny'd,
damnify'd, discours'd, divulg'd, dy'd, endur'd, endeavour'd, enter'd,

---

[1] Cf. Miège. Op. cit. p. 82. "L'*e* se convertit souvent en apostrophe, pour
réduire par là deux syllabes en une:—*lov'd, amus'd, esteem'd; mark't,* et *marked;
imbraced* et *imbrac't.*"

ex cus'd, expell'd, extoll'd, harbour'd, honour'd, mov'd, imbalm'd, p ractiz'd, prais'd, propos'd, pleas'd, presum'd, question'd, reckon'd (twice), reform'd, releas'd, referr'd, reply'd, scrupl'd, seis'd, setl'd, s uffic'd, sway'd, treasur'd, troubl'd, try'd, unbridl'd, unlicenc'd, unprincipl'd, unedify'd, us'd, utter'd, view'd.—L. to H.:—constrain'd, continu'd, describ'd, enlarg'd, extoll'd, lesson'd, obtain'd, prevail'd, pleas'd, practiz'd, receiv'd, train'd, turmoil'd, unprincipl'd, untutor'd, wander'd.—Acced. Comm. Grammar:—call'd, chang'd, compar'd, declin'd (2), diriv'd (2), form'd, joyn'd (3), prais'd, us'd.—Doct. and Disc. of Div. I.:—attain'd, describ'd, despis'd, deny'd, disturb'd, exclaim'd, fear'd, happn'd, observ'd, receiv'd, parabl'd, scrupl'd, us'd, ser'd, stigmatiz'd; III.:—answer'd, annull'd, free'd, reliev'd, satisfy'd.

6. Final *d* was changed into *t,* after the dropping of *e,* in verbs ending in a sharp consonant:—

a) *Sharp labials (p, f).* Areop.:—Ript up, stopt.—D. and D. of Div.:—Stopt.

b) *Sharp palatals (c, k[ck], ch* [in church]). Ram. 38, askt.— C. P. B. 221, toucht.—Anim. 15, stretch't.—Areop.:—fabrict, bewicht, provokt.—L. to H.:—mockt, coucht.—D. and D. of Div.:—lookt.

c) *Sharp sibilants (s, sh, [x], c).*

α) *s.*—Ram. 38, repulst.—Areop.:—dispers't, mist, repulst, profest, supprest.—L. to H.:—discourst, prest.—Acced. Comm. Grammar:—encreast.—D. and D. of Div.:—confes't, expres't.

β) *sh.*—Ram. 37, banisht.—C. P. B. 74, punisht.—Anim. 11, gash't. — Areop.:—banish't, establisht, publisht, punisht.— Acced. Comm. Grammar.:—diminisht.—D. and D. of Div.:—extinguisht.

γ) *c (x).* Ram. 40, forc't, seduc't.—C. P. B. 179, reduc't.— Areop.: —intermixt, licenc't, produc't, mixt, plac't.—L. to H.:—induc't, reduc't.—D. and D. of Div.:—divorc't, forc't.

7. Verbs ending in *d* or *t* regularly take *ed,* according to present use. Ex.:—Ram. 37, revolted; 38, founded.—C. P. B. 220, permited.—Areop.:—affected, appointed, corrupted, delighted, dreaded, printed, slighted, indetted.—L. to H.:—digested, presented, reputed.—Acced. Comm. Grammar:—compounded.

8. *Past participles,* used as adjectives, likewise take *ed* and do not drop *e,* which proves that the final syllable was sounded as it is to-day in learnéd, a learnéd man. Areop.:—Armed men; a deceased author; confused seeds; the reformed citty; a rejected Truth;—substantive:—the number of their damned.—L. to H.:—Men of approved wisdom; learned correspondence; (the past participle of the verb "to learn" occurs regularly as:—learnt; in Ram. too, and C. P. B. learn't); renowned authors; ragged notions.

9. *Mute e* is omitted in the ending *en:*—Ram. 38, drivn; 39, faln.—Areop.:—writt'n, giv'n; to happ'n, it happ'ns, to lik'n, it betok'ns.—L. to H.:—spok'n, silk'n, fal'n; to disburd'n, disburd'ning.—Eikon. 5, ridd'n, beat'n, forgott'n; so also entring, hindring. It is dropped in words like bowr, drunk'ness, cov'nant, cov'nanting, the midd'st, ev'n; in compounds like:—houshold, in which O. E. *hús,* M. E. *hous* may have influenced the spelling; in the compounds of *som:*—somwhere, somtimes, somwhat; in formost, O. E. *formesta, fyrmesta,* M. E. *formest,* superlative of *"forme;"* modern *e* (foremost) is therefore etymologically not justifiable; in the compounds of where, there, here:—wherof, wherin, wherwith; therfore, therin, therby; heerby.—Weak final *e* is omitted in the plurals:—Proviso's, limbo's (Areop.). Weak *o* even is replaced by an apostrophe in reck'n'd, pris'ner, so *i* in ord'nary.

10. In Herbert, Hobbes and Browne, the omission of weak *e* has become very rare. We have noted the forms:—enricht, marcht, in Herbert; stockt, and burnt, in Browne; and in Taylor we found:—α. bettred, christned, remembred; β. dasht, design'd, and far'd, fixt, sweld, remembred.

B. y, ie.

Peculiar, too, in Milton and in the writers of the first half of the XVIIth century, is the unsettled orthography of words (chiefly of French origin) ending in *y, ie.* Sweet states that the writing of *y* for *i* was carried to great lengths in Early Mn. English. " *Y* or *ie* was always written finally, as in *many, manie, citie,* but otherwise the two letters were written almost at random."[1] He goes on to explain that this use of *ie* is the result of the weakening of M. E. *ie* in such words as *melodíe, melody, chivalríe,* which, at the end of the M. E. period, drew back the stress from the ending.

In old French the stress generally fell on the same syllable as in Latin, i. e. a word was either paroxytonon or proparoxytonon; but, through the dropping of final Latin syllables, many French words came to have the stress on the last syllable, as in *honoúr,* Lat. honórem; *pitíé,* Lat. pietátem.—When first introduced into M. E., French words kept their original stress:—*natúre, honoúr, pitíe.* Such words, however, afterwards threw the stress back on to the first syllable, by the analogy of the native English words, such as:— *fáder, bódy,* becoming *náture, píty.*—Now weak final *e* in words ending in *ie* could be dropped, *i* was shortened, and the ending could be written indifferently *ie* or *y*.

1. That in Milton *y* was written at random for *i,* may be shown by his spelling the present participle ending *-ing,* sometimes *-yng* and sometimes *-ing.* In one and the same sentence (Doct. and Disc. of Div., Cap. II) we find the forms:—claimyng, visiting, stepping. (Areop. satyricall=satiricall).

2. As to the words ending in *y* (present English), we notice in Milton a greater uniformity than in other writers of his time. We may say that, as a rule, nouns corresponding to French substantives ending in *té* (tatem) are spelt *ty.* Instances of *ie* are extremely rare. So we have:—Ram. 40, solemnity, but 38, chastitie, inchastitie; C. P. B. 160, prosperity, 182, authority; 191, cruelty, dignity (twice); 221, necessity, privity;—Prel. Episc.:—authority;—R. of Ch. G.:— society;—Eikon.:—divinity;—Areop.:—autority, capacity, city, falsity (fausseté), fidelity, impunity, infallibility, ingenuity, liberty, necessity, piety, satiety (satiété);– Col.:—autority, charity, contrariety, deputy, diversity, divinity, familiarity, liberty, necessity, sincerity, university;—L. to H.:—brevity, capacity;—Doct. and Disc. of Div.:—antiquity, dignity, iniquity;—Acced. Comm. Gr.:—quantity, quality. On the other hand we have:—Ram. 39, Monodie, mercie, constancie; 37, clergie, companie, tragedie, tyrannie; 38, beggery, clergy, ladie; 40,

---

[1] Sweet. Op. cit. 267.

frequency; victorie; 41, journie, victorie;—C. P. B. 74, magistracie; 109, clergie, fury, prelacie; 181, dutie; 182, clergie, tyrannie; 191, insolencie; 220, storie, subsidie; 221, a ladie, his policie; 242, armie; 244, storie; 220 and 221, repeatedly:—monie and mony (never money), monies;—Areop.:—adversarie, controversie, fancie (French fantaisie), efficacie, heresie, politie, potencie, prophesie;—Col.:—anatomie;—L. to H.:—(authoritie), controversie, difficultie, puritie;—D. and Disc. of Div. I, christianitie, civilitie; IV, charitie; VI, hypocrisie;—VII, necessitie, antiquitie;—Acc. Comm. Gr.:—etymologie, penaltie;—Anim. 8, anatomie; 9, oratory; 10, civil politie; 12, episcopacy;—Prel. Episc.:—episcopacy, sufficiency, vice-gerency;—Eikon. 5, mediocritie; 6, libertie; 8, politie; 10, Breviary, clergie.—In most of these cases we can trace French influence.

Adjectives are to be found with both spellings, *y* and *ie*. Easy and easie; fiery and fierie; ayrie, pecuniary, mercenary; adv. easily.

Verbs are spelt indiscriminately with *y* and *ie*. To satisfie and satisfy, to sanctifie and sanctify.

3. Mulcaster's "Elementarie" gives us a clue to the comprehension of this spelling. We find in it the following explanation:—

"*i* hath a form somtime vowellish, somtime consonantish. In the vowellish sound either it endeth a former syllable, or the verie last. When it endeth the last, and is it self the last letter, if it sound gentlie it is qualified by the *e* as:—*manie, merie,* when the verie pen will rather end in *e* than in the naked *i*. If it sound sharp and loud, it is to be written *y*, having no *e* after it, as neding no qualification:—*deny, cry, defy.*"[1] "*Y*" then sounds "sharp and loud" when the accent rests upon it; Mulcaster, at least, does not give any other examples; in these cases Milton, too, writes *y*. Ex. Col.:—They ly heer; try'd, cry'd, deny'd.—But in adjectives, and in most substantives (except those in *ty*) in which the *i* sound is gentle, the spelling *ie* prevails.

Butler (Grammar; p. 10) explains that "*y* being a Greek vowel is rightly used every where in words originally Greek, as *crystall, polypus,* and common use hath allowed it in the ending of other English words:—in so much that *i* and *y* are in that place used

---

[1] Cf. Ellis. Op. cit. III, 913.

indifferently, but *i* more in substantives and verbs, as:—*bounti, commoditi, a lie, to trie, to die, to lie* (unless it make a diphtong as in *ey, they, may, say*), and *y* more in adjectives and adverbs, as *my, thy, why, by, many, twenty, godly, humbly.* Also when two *ii* come together, *y* hath commonly the place of the former, *burying, marrying, dying."*

Hodges ("Special Considerations," § 5, 6,) allows both ways of spelling, saying, however, that *y* ought to be alone used in words of Greek origin; all substantives should end in *ie:*—*cittie, dittie, bellie,* and all adverbs and adjectives in *y;* and he himself follows that rule.

In Bullokar's "Expositor," 1616, words ending in *y* (subst., adj. and adv.) are an exception. So under *A* we find 3 words ending in *y*:—adulatory, affability, agony, and 24 other words in *ie; B, C, D,* have no words in *y,* and 8, 26, 16 words ending in *ie.— I* has relatively the greatest number, 8 in *y* and 14 in *ie,* but *E, F, G, H,* have none, with 16, 6, 6, 8 respectively in *ie.*

Fifty years later, among the most important reforms of the XVIIth century, Miège mentions also the fact that the ending *ie* has been reduced to *y:*—"Et de fait on n'écrit plus guère aujourd'hui: *jealousie, easie, to denie,* mais presque toujours *y."* Yet:—"On a changé *y* en *i* dans:—*mine, thine,* cependant on écrit encore indifféremment: *aid, ayd, boyl* et *boil."*

In Hewes "Perfect Survey" there is a chapter on:—"Certain considerations fit for our young Latines," in which the author gives a few rules which may prove helpful to the young learner, to remember the Latin words. The English words ending in *ty* correspond to Latin words in *tas, acc. tátem,* and this is what we notice in Milton.

In Coote's "Vocabulary," edition of 1662, the words ending in Mod. E. in *y* have already that ending, with the exception of the 13 following:—*apostasie, to exemplifie, fantasie, gratifie, lapidarie, to justifie, leprosie, maladie, to mortifie, phrensie, to prophesie, to putrifie, to ratifie.*

4. As regards the spelling of the Preterite and Past Participle of verbs ending in *y,* it is unsettled in Milton's prose. We have met forms in *y,* preceded by a consonant, deny'd. Present orthography would require, at least, deni'd.—D. and D. of Div.:—satisfy'd, but also:—undeified, betraied, and even (Acc. Comm. Gr.) applyed.— Col.:—marryed.

5. Adverbs in *ly* are generally written according to present use. Col.:—justly, manly, unfitly, very, frequently, universally.—Areop.:— usually, dubiously, darkly, nicely, passionately.—L. to H.:—assuredly, delightfully, easily, partly, lastly, &c.

6. Milton's contemporaries seem to have adopted Mulcaster's, Butler's and Hodges' rules, for, in the great majority of cases, they spell *ie* at the end of words, wherever *i* (*y*) sounds "gentlie." So:—Bacon, Cam. Ser. I.:—abilitie, armie, conformitie, libertie, partie, propertie, posteritie, territorie; adject.:—haughtie, easie, mightie. H' VII. Cam. Ser. 2:—inquirie, majestie, nobilitie, partie (rarely *y*, plenty, penury), monie. Ad. of. L.:—anxietie (2), arrogancie, bodie, capacitie (3), charitie, difficultie, dignitie, dutie, glorie, enquirie, excellencie (4), facilitie (2), felicitie, historie, jealousie, magnanimitie, malignitie, majestie (4), memorie, philosophie, proprietie, qualitie, quantitie (2), severitie, summarie, triplicitie, universalitie, varietie, ventositie; adj· happie, ordinarie, unworthie; (*y* in enquiry, glory, impossibility, propriety; all adverbs in *ly*).—Herbert, Hist. of G.:—beautie (2), bodie, dexteritie, envie, impietie, innocencie, integritie, mortalitie, pietie, pittie, posteritie, royaltie, tragedie, varietie, villanie, (idolatry, itinerary, tyranny, victory; adj. unworthy; adv. in *ly*).—Taylor has already adopted the ending *y; ie* occurs but rarely. α. Subst. assembly, plur. assemblyes, authority (always), capacity, charity, directory, excellency, incompetency, integrity, liturgy (once:—liturgie), offertory (es), piety; adj.:—hasty, holy, ordinary; verbs:—to satisfie; adverbs throughout in *ly*.—β. Subst. charity (2), cruelty, dyscrasy, mercy (3), society, study, tyranny; adj. contrary, but busie (2); adv. presently.—Hobbes has both endings, Hu. Nat.:—subst. anatomy, body, impossibility, quality, but controversie (2), imagerie; adj. necessary (3); adv. in *ly*, easily. Lib. of Subj., Cam. Ser.:— assemblie, equitie, immunitie, iniquitie, libertie (9); rarely *y*, assembly, liberty, democraty. Dissolution of a Commonwealth. Cam. Ser.:— citie, epilepsie, pleurisie, crasie.

Browne, on the other hand, keeps *y* chiefly in substantives:— Ur. B. antiquity (2), discovery (2), reality, society, but *effigie;* adj. and adverbs in *y*, *ly:* — fiery, deeply, frequently, indifferently, strictly, totally. But verbs:—to lie, to satisfie.

Whenever it sounded "sharp and loud," they used the spelling indicated by Mulcaster:—*y,* or added the qualifying *e,* as Bacon does in:—amplifie, &c.; Hobbes, Lib. of S., Cam. Ser.:—applyed. lyeth, tyed; Dissol. of a Com., Cam. Ser.:—dyeth, implyeth, signifie, style, supplyed.—Browne has:—Rel. Med.:—we lye; Urne Bur.:—dyed (died), to dye (die), lye.—Taylor spells:—emptyed, they prophesyed. All these writers also used *y* for *i* at random in the body of words. Milton, Ram. 39:—voiage, choysest; 40, journy; 31, poyson'd, dyes, tyme; C. P. B. 185, poyson, voiage; – Bible:—dyed;—Bacon:— choyce, sayd, spoyled;—Hobbes writes:—chayns and chains, poyson, joyning;—Dissol. Cam. Ser.:—nayles, fayries, entrayls;—Browne:— U. B. the ayr, oyntment, dayly, to avoyd, coynes;—Taylor:—veynes, assoylment, imployment, voyces, choycest;—Hobbes spells:—mony;— Herbert:—aymed, ayding, countrey, joynes, vayled=veiled.

C. The sound ē.

The sound ē, such as it is found in the personal pronouns *he, me,* can be represented in modern English by different spellings:— 1. *e:*—he, me; 2. *ee:*—to see; 3. *ei:*—to receive; 4. *ie:*—to believe; 5. *ea:*—the sea.

1. Now Milton, in common with the other writers of the period, shows a tendency to adopt a uniform spelling *ee,* which is prevailing in many places in his writings.—

Milton's spelling is as follows:—

Rambl. a) *ee* prevails, so *ie=ee,* in theefe (37 and 72), but we find also:

    b) *ea=ei* in 37, to receave.

    c) *ie* is rendered by *ei* regularly in the words beseidging, feild, preist; verb:—to greive.

C. P. B. a) *ee=ea* in 19, cleerly.

    b) *ie* is rendered by *ei* in 53, cheifest; 179, cheife; 109, preists (2); 185, mischeif (2).—Bi. *ec=ē* in eevning, (1646).

Eikon. a) *ee*‥ē in wee, heer (3).

    b) *ee=ea* in neerest.

    c) *ee=ie* in greevance.

    d) *ie* again is generally interverted:—feirce (3), to beleive.

Areop. a) ē is rendered by *ee,* in the pronouns:—wee, yee, hee (and also we, ye, he), in to bee, "it will bee," in meer, meerly, heer. Bacon, Taylor, Hobbes and Browne also spell:—hee, mee, wee, bee, meere, meer.

b) ēā is rendered by *ee* throughout in:—neer; year is mostly spelt yeer. Bacon has:—leese, yeeres;—Hobbes:—deerly, cleerer;—Browne:—the rere (to bring up).

c) *ie* is rendered by *ee* throughout in:—peece (a peece of framework, hewd into peeces), whereas the peace, Lat. *pax,* is always spelt with *ea;* beleeve (4).

Herbert has also:—to beleeve; Browne:—beleeve, theef, a peece of folly.—We find however the forms:—theam; compleatly, unweildy, leige. (Browne:—compleat). Modern:—*"fever"* is repeatedly spelt feaver, feavor (Bacon:—feaver), though it never contained an *ea.* O. E. *féfor, fefer.*

Colast. a) ē is rendered by *ee* in:—hee, mee, wee, yee, to bee, eev'n, heer, heerby.

b) ēā is rendered by *ee* in:—cleerly, neer.

c) *ie* is rendered by *ee* in:—greevance, peece, to beleeve.— Yet *ei* is rendered by *ea* in:—to conceave, to deceav, to perceav, to receav, received; again *ie* by *ei* in:—breifly, cheif, mischeif, yeilds, freinds.

L. to H. a) *ee* = ē in:—heer, meere, meerly.

b) *ee*=ēā in:—cleer, cleerly, neer, neerest, yeer.

c) *ee*=*ie* in peece, peeces.—Again ēā=ē in extreame, extreamly, theams. *ei*—*ie* in beseiging. "To teach" is spelt according to present use.

Doct. and Disc. of Div. a) *ee*=ē in:—to bee, meer.

b) *ee*—*ie* in:—beleef, greevance, peece; but:—relief; and ea e in compleat, extreame, discreat.

Bacon spells:—yeeres, but:—extreame, supreame.—Herbert has:—cleerer, deer, neere.—Taylor:—to beleeve (2); but:—years, regularly.—Hobbes:—meerly, neerly.—Browne has regularly:—years, too, and neare, but:—beleevers, to beleeve, meere (yet:—neare).

We see that there was much hesitation between the spellings ee and ēa, both existed and were often used indiscriminately in the XVIIth century.

2. The following peculiarities may also be taken note of. Milton regularly writes:—freind, freinds (his sonnets are all to his "freinds").

Modern *been* is mostly found spelt:—bin, in accordance with its short pronunciation.

The sound *ei,* in modern *"their,"* is generally rendered by a simple *i:*—thir, thire, throughout in the MSS., Eikon., Col., Areop., L. to H., Acced. Comm. Gr. This may lead us to conclude that the word was pronounced like mod.:—*fir,* to *stir,* where the presence of the *r* brings about what the Germans call "Trübung" of the vowel sound. Cf. C. P. B. 181, concerning; 109, hire (her).

In "frontispice" (Areop.) we have the correcter orthography; the word comes from the Latin *frontispicium* (specio); the vulgar spelling is due to an erroneous notion that the latter part of the word is connected with:—*piece.* [1]

3. *ĕă,* according to Ellis I., 86, generally represented the sound *e* in *led* (pret. of "to lead"); this is what may have induced the writers to adopt the spelling:—*neer, cleer,* in order to avoid confusion.—Milton avoids *ĕă,* and writes according to pronunciation:— to spred, the dispredders of vice, steddy, a steddy pace (L. to H.), lerned, learning and lerning (Ar. and Col.). (Bacon writes both:— spread and spred.) Ram.:—lerned. (Herbert:—endevoring. Taylor:—endevours.)

4. The sound *ai,* in mod.:—*claim,* is rendered by a simple ā in words of Romance origin; this is no doubt rather a phonetic than an etymological spelling. Ex.:—Areop.:—proclame, proclam'd.

D. o, oa, ou.

Here again a tendency to simplify makes itself felt. Present oā was rendered by ō. Ram. 39:—bemoning; Areop.:—cote, inrodes, rodes. (Bacon:—othes;—Herbert:—fome;—Browne:—grone). On

---
[1] Cf. Hales. Areop. 106.

the other hand ō is rendered by oä in Areop.:—yoak. (Hobbes: — aboad; — Herbert: — cloaths; — Browne: — stroaks of affliction; — Hobbes H. N.:—stroak [27].) *Choose* is found spelt *chuse*. M. E. had the forms *chusen* and *chesen* (O. E. *ceosan*). Likewise *cruise* is spelt *cruse; bruised=brus'd.* — Herbert spells:—he will chuse.

We find in Ram. 40, the door spelt:—dore; 41, plough spelt:— plow, plowman; C. P. B. Soldier is written throughout with *ou*, souldier, souldiers, and we notice the following spellings:—74, 160, amoung; 111, 220, daunce, dauncing; 221, cozin.—Bi.:—half an hower (1648), wedensday (1652). Anim.: —a shoo; the shoar; clarks; sammon; Iland.—All these words are instances of phonetic spelling. In maister (Anim. 15), the Lat. *i* has remained, Lat.:—*magister*.

Bacon has:—Adv. of L. commaundements, the woonder, the fourme of the temptation, daunger, particulers.—Herbert (Hist. of Geo.):—bloud, bloudshed, murther.—Hobbes:—thorow (2), councel.—Taylor:—bloodshed, shoar, souldiers.—Browne:—burthen.

We may conclude our remarks on vowels by quoting the following statements made by Miège in his Introductory Remarks, to which we have referred already. Among the changes that have gone on in the XVIIth century, "*burthen, murther,*" says he, "sont devenus *burden, murder; ea* est devenu ē: — *compleat, extream, supream; oa* est abandonné, donc on écrit:—*smoke, cloke, sope, fole, grone, moneful, rost*, qui ont meilleure grâce que:—*smoak, cloak, soap, foal, groan*, &c. Pour ne pas multiplier les choses sans nécessité, il vaut mieux écrire *mony, hony, peny, chance, gard, month, sum*. On écrit aussi *ie*, au lieu de *ei, ee*, dans *field, piece, yield, thief; ou*, au lieu de *oo*, dans:—*bloud, floud.*"

E. Consonants.

1. In "suttle, suttlest" found repeatedly in Areop. and Col., we have another instance of phonetic spelling, while the present:— *subtle* instances etymological spelling. In M. E. the forms were *sotel, sotile, soutil*, and *subtil*. Old French: *—soutil, sutil;* the *b* is due to the Latin word *subtilis.*—A similar case is:—dettors, indetted (Areop.), Lat. *debitum;*—perfet (Areop.), Fr. *parfait* was made into *parfaict* by the influence of Latin:—*perfectum.*

2. *s* and *c* are occasionally interchanged. Milton spells:—recompense and recompence, license and licence, without regard to the difference in the meaning of the words. In our days we should take *licence* to mean a permission granted, whereas *license* means the abusive use of the permission given, of rights or privileges. Similarly:—expence and expense, choisest, scars (Doct. and Disc. of Div.).—Areop.:—fansy, fansied; this spelling comes nearer to the original *"phantasy,"* of which *fancy* is a contracted form.—Ram. 79, choysest;—C. P. B. 186, the expences; 221, devises;—Eikon.:—his own chois.—Bacon:—Adv. of L. sences (2).

Regarding the endings *ense* and *ence,* Hodges (Special Consid., § 7) declares that *ence* is to be used in substantives only, as:—a sence, a recompence, and *ense* in verbs, to sense, to recompense.

3. Sonorous *s* and *z,* too, are interchanged; we have seen above:—practiz'd, stigmatiz'd, seis'd, but:—the practise, &c.

4. The use of *v* and *u* is settled in Milton; one exception to the rules of present orthography has been found in:—perswade, which is repeatedly spelt so, in all pamphlets.—In his contemporaries' writings *u* is still prevailing. Bacon writes for instance:—reuenuew, graue, obseruation, deserue, haue, suruey, ouer.—Herbert and Browne have:—perswade, euery houre;—Taylor:—discouery, perswaded.

Miège (Introd.):—"On emploie indifféremment *u* et *w:—dissuade, disswade."*

F. Prefixes.

1. Even in present English there is no fixed rule as to the use of the French prefix *en, em, in, im.* It is mainly a verbformer. The French form of this prefix is *en, em,* preserved in English in such words as:—*endure, engaged, employ.* But in many words of French introduction the Latin form has been restored, as in:—*indite* (M. E. *endíten*), *inquire, imprint.*

As the spelling makes no difference in the pronunciation, it fluctuates in some words between the Latin and French forms.[1]—

---

[1] Sweet. Op. cit. 474.

Milton makes more frequent use of the Latin form. Ex.:—Areop. imbalmed, to imploy, imployment (Col.:—imploiment), to indear, indear'd, to inable, to disinable;—D. and D. of Div.:—inabled, disinabled, to intice, inticing, to indanger (run danger);—R. of Ch. G.:—intirely.—But:—Acced. Comm. Gr.:—to encrease, encreast; so Ba., Ad. of L.:—imbraced;—Herbert, Hist. of Geo.:—ingagement;—Taylor:—ingaged, imployment. But Hobbes:—encreased; Browne:—enquirers.

Miège says:—"On emploie indifféremment *em* et *in*:—*employment, imployment.*"

2. The English prefix *be* is found in:—bejesuited (Areop.); belawgiv'n (D. and D. of Div.); beknave, befriend, bejade (Anim.). This is the same word as the preposition *be, bv,* whose strong form is the adverb *by;* both the adverb and the prefix at first meant:—about, around. The most general function of *be* is now to specialize the meaning of transitive verbs, as in *besettan,* beset, and to make an intransitive verb transitive:—*bewépan,* to bewail, bepencan, to consider.

G. Suffixes.

1. In "wedloc" (Col. repeatedly) we have the etymological spelling of the English suffix *lác,* from the O. E. noun:—*lác,* whose ordinary meaning is "gift," "sacrifice," but which shows traces of the older meanings "game, fight," agreeing with those of the verb *lácan,* to play; *wedlac* (*wedd* "pledge, contract"). The *o* of "wedloc" was long in M. E.; it has been shortened in modern English, and to this is due the spelling *locc, lock.* (The doubling of a final consonant as a sign of shortness of the preceding vowel has been discussed above.) In Milton's time the *o* was still long. [1]

2. The spelling of the Latin suffix *ic* (icus, Gr. ικός) is unsettled in Milton. We meet forms like these:—Areop.:—public, publick, publicke, laick, hereticks, pedantick;—Anim. 17:—physick, logick; C. P. B.:—catholick.—The latter forms *ck,* however, were gradually disappearing in Milton's time; the forms in *ic* are growing in number.—Johnson, a century later, attempted to reintroduce *ck,* but

---

1 Sweet. Op. cit. 462.

towards the end of the XVIIIth century it was dropped again. [1]—
We notice great hesitation as to the adoption of one common spelling; some writers, like Bacon and Browne, kept *ck* evidently as a
phonetic spelling to denote shortness of preceding vowel, according
to the well-known rule of double consonants. Bacon:—fabrick.—
Hobbes, H. N.:—logick, optick (4), politick (2), rhetorick.—Browne,
Cam. Ser.:—collick, ethicks, rhetoricke, scepticks, stoicks, to prog-
nostick, authentick, logick, musick, politickly, publick.—Others, like
Hobbes and Taylor, preferred the French spelling *que,* which is
occasionally found in Bacon, never in Milton.—Bacon has (Cam.
Ser.:—politique, publique; Adv. of L.:—politiques (politicians), Arch-
herctiques.—Herbert, Hist. of Geo.:—reliques.—Taylor, α. publike
(3); β. publick, heretique.—Hobbes, Cam. Ser.:—politique, publique, ecclesiastiques, publiquely.—Taylor:—catholiques.—Browne,
U. B.:—reliques.

Coote says, part II, p. 25:—"To know when a word endeth
in *like,* publicke, when in *que,* as oblique, is hard without the Latine
tongue from whence most of them be borrowed," and he gives the
following rule in the margin:—"When you have a word derived of
a Latine word which endeth in (cus) write (like) as in publike, from
publicus. But when a word is derived from a Latin word ending in
(quus) write (que) as oblique from obliquus, but traffique with (que),
because it is French."

Coote did not know that the endings *cus, quus* are identical;—
antiquus is spelt *anticus* by Ennius and Livy. [2]—*qu* seems to be
developed out of *c.* [3] Coote then goes on:—"We write *publike* because we say *publication,* for *c* and *k* here be both one, so *rhetorick,*
because we say *rhetorician.*"—A rule so confuse was not easily followed, and Miège is wiser when he simply says that *ck* and *k* can be
used indifferently at the end of words in *ick.* (II. Partie. Chap. I.
Des Mots et des Sentences.)

---

[1] Rost. Die Orthographie der ersten Quartoausgabe von Milton's Par. Lost.
Leipzig, Diss. 1892.

[2] Cf. Georges. Lexicon der lat. Wortformen, s. v. antiquus.

[3] Schweizer-Sidler. Lat. Gramm., § 4. "*qu* ist weder ein Doppelconsonant,
noch eine Silbe, sondern lautet wie *c* mit labialem Nachklang."—Cf. also:—Brugg-
mann. Vergleichende Grammatik. II. 1. 241 and 238, § 84.

Hodges agrees on the whole with Coote (Spec. Observ., § 2, p. 17), yet he finds that in words like *back, neck,* c and k are not both needed, and that either the one letter or the other might be dropped, but "custom" will have both.

3. The Latin suffix *or* (Lat. or) *our* (ōrem), old French ŏr.—It is a personal suffix. The fact that *or* had the same sound as *er* explains such a spelling as:—instructer (Areop.).—In Latin this ending is preceded by derivative *t,* which, under certain conditions, becomes *s:*—imperator, professor.[1] C. P. B. 179, governours; 183, emperour.— In old French the *t* was dropped, leaving a hiatus as in:—*empereor, sauveor.* Hence the E. Mn. English forms:—emperour, autour, gouvernour (Areop.); yet:—Eikon. fevor, rumor, rigor (and rigour). This *our* is now spelt *or,* except in:—*saviour.* But in Milton's time *our* still prevailed. Miège II, 1, also keeps it. Bacon, Cam. Ser.:— counsellours, governours, emperours, inferiour and superiour; Adv. of L.:—Emperour (2), mirrour (humors). —Herbert, Hist. of Geo.: — dolours, horrour, predecessours, saviour; adj. inferiour (but endevoring). —Taylor: — superiour, exteriour. — Hobbes, Cam. Ser.:— William the Conquerour; H. N.: —exteriour, interiour.—Browne:— counsellours (in:—observators, the Latin ending remained unchanged).

4. Another Latin suffix *or, our* (Lat. or, ōrem) forms abstract nouns, chiefly from verbs. In Mn. E. the French spelling *our* is preferred to the Latin *or,* especially in popular words. In Milton the forms *or* and *our* are to be found. Areop.:—armor, honor, humor; L. to H.:—ardor, humors; but:—errour; Doct. and Disc. of Div.:— vigor, rigor; Col.:—rumor, honour. — Bacon writes throughout: — errour, favour, honour, splendour, succour. — Hobbes: — errour, terrour.

5. Mention must be made here of the great uncertainty prevailing in the spelling of the suffix *ness.* O. E. *ness, niss, nyss.* Goth. *nassus.* O. H. G.:—*nassi, nissi, nissa;* M. H. G.:—*nisse;* N. H. G.:—*niss.* It is the regular ending for forming abstract nouns: — *a)* from adjectives:—gōdnis, *goodness, greatness; b)* from substantives as:— *witness, wilderness,* O. E. *wildeorness; c)* from Romance adjectives

---

[1] Sweet. N. E. G. 480.

ending in *able, al, ant, ar, ary, ate, able, ible, ic, ous.*—We find it spelt in various ways, in Milton:—*nesse, ness, nes.*—The form *nes* is predominant, then comes the form *nesse*, and the form *ness*, which is alone in use now, occurs rarely. Ram. 39, sicknesse, but 38, slackness; 40, buisness; C. P. B. 17, beastlines; 111, boldnes; but 17, drunkennesse; 180, earnestnesse; 179, forwardnesse; 191, licentiousnesse; 58, filthynisse exemplifies the M. E. ending *nisse;* Areop.:—aptnes, backwardnes, finenes, forwardnes (twice), happines, lovelines, meeknes, newnes, plainnes, profusenes, remissenes, roughnes, softnes, statelines, strictnes, unsutablenes, weaknes (twice), wearines, witnes (and witnesse). On the other hand we have:—businesse, cheerfulnesse, contentednesse, covetousnesse, darknesse, exactnesse, fearfulnesse, goodnesse, rashnesse, ripenesse, sharpnesse, surlinesse, voluptuousnesse, uprightnesse, uncorruptednesse, witnesse, warinesse, whitenesse; not one form in *ness;*—Col.:—madnes, perversnes, rudenes, sharpnes, unfitnes, unhappines, watchfulnes, weaknes, wildernes, wretchednes.—But.:—carelessness, vastness, readiness.— L. to H.:—exactnesse, grossnesse, harshnesse, sullennesse, warinesse;—D. and Disc. of Div., Cap. I:—nakednes, strictnes, unfitnes, weaknes;—but:—goodnesse, uncleannesse; II, remotenes, solitarines, but:—loneliness, solitariness; III, wearinesse; IV, prophetesse and muteness, unlivelyness; VI, sadnesse; VII, cheerefulnesse, unpreparednesse.

There seems to be more uniformity in the other writers of the period which we have compared with Milton. In the passages from Bacon, Herbert, Jeremy Taylor, Hobbes, and Browne, we have not found one form in *nes,* nor one in *ness.* Ba., Ad. of L.:— businesse, carefulnesse, cheerefulnesse, darknesse, faithfulnesse, fulnesse, largenesse, readinesse, shortnesse, strangenesse, swiftnesse.—Herbert (Hist. of Geo.):—darknesse, happinesse, weaknesse.—Taylor:—α. bitternesse, finenesse, goodnesse, sharpnesse, β. gentlenesse (3), greedinesse, forgivenesse, madnesse, meeknesse, quicknesse.—Hobbes, H. N., has:—highness.

The spelling *nesse* was then, if not universally used, at least far predominant.—We notice, moreover, that the greater number of substantives formed by means of the suffix *ness* are polysyllabic, and generally bear the stress on the last syllable but two, which is, as a rule, the root syllable; ex.:—háppiness, búsiness, unprepáredness. Now we may distinguish three main degrees of stress or loudness:—strong, half-strong or medium, and weak. Thus, in *"háppiness"* the first syllable is strong, the second is week, then the tone rises again and the last syllable, *ness,* is half-strong, or bears a secondary stress. This fact that a second vocal effort has to be made in pronouncing the ending, renders the sudden stopping of the breath, that is to say the sharp pronunciation of the flat sibilant *s* considerably more difficult than if the syllable had but a weak stress, and were not accentuated, as in *"glorious, joyous."* This may explain why the less educated classes of our days, finding some difficulty in the sharp pronunciation of words ending in a flat consonant, seem to be sounding a weak final *e* after words like:—*cup, lock, bat, brass,* or after monosyllabic nouns containing a lengthened vowel:—*dog(ge), fear(e), loaf(e), pain(e), bread(e), Lord(e).* That is, of course, not the case in words like:— *London, letter, baker,* whose last syllable is but weakly sounded.—This same difficulty was experienced in Milton's time, and pronunciation alone can account for the spelling *nesse.*

We stated above that the present pronunciation of English is mainly due to the orthoepists of the XVIIIth and XIXth centuries, while in the XVIIth century many words were sounded in a style which we now should generally condemn, so we may be certain that Bacon was writing quite in accordance with his pronunciation when he spelt (Cam. Ser.):—Businesse, greatnesse, happinesse, closenesse, privatenesse, softnesse, strangenesse, sweetnesse; so also Hobbes (Cam. Ser.):—darknesse, greatnesse, readinesse, sicknesse;—Herbert (Cam. Ser.):—covetousnesse, darknesse;—Browne (Cam. Ser.):—unworthinesse, darknesse, happinesse, nearnesse.—Taylor (Cam. Ser.):—businesse, goodnesse, lawfulnesse, unaptnesse, weaknesse, willingnesse.

And now, if we return to Milton, we see that, conscious as he was of the short character of *e* in *ness,* he wrote as his own experience and knowledge of the language led him to do—doubling the final consonant to denote shortness,—but that he could not avoid being influenced by the pronunciation on the one hand, and by his contemporaries' orthography on the other.

6. The same may be said of the suffix *ess,* French *esse,* from Latin *issa,* which denotes female persons.—Ramb. 39:—Goddesse; C. P. B. 109:—Marquesse (fem. of marquis); 179, the Empresse.

7. Substantives formed by means of the suffix *dom* (O. E. *dŏm*= judgment, authority, in combination with adjectives expresses "condition" generally), are to be found sometimes with qualifying *e,* sometimes without *e.* So for instance:—Ram. 40:—wisdome;— Areop.:—wisdome and wisdom, kingdome, martyrdome;—Doct. and Disc. of Div.:—thraldome, wisdome. The spelling *"dome,"* found in every pamphlet, is prevailing.

Bacon writes throughout:—wisedome;—Herbert,Hist.of Geo.:— martyrdome;—Jeremy Taylor:—kingdome; α, wisedome, Christendome (α and β);—Hobbes has:—freedome and freedom, and fredome. He drops the *e* in the plural of:— kingdoms (6 times in Dissol. of a Commonw., Cam. Ser.).—Browne has (Rel. Med., Cam. Ser.):— wisedom.

The pronunciation of the word was apparently unsettled; some pronounced the adj. *wise* fully, and added *dom,* which, receiving a secondary stress, had its vowel lengthened, hence:—*dome;* while others pronounced *wis* short, then *dom, dome,* remembering perhaps the originally long nature of the *o.*

8. The suffix *ure,* Latin ūra, generally preceded by derivative *t, (s),* has been used by Milton in forming the collective word "serviture" (Ramb. 40), in the sense of "the servants."

9. Uncertainty prevails in the writing of the adjective forming suffix *less* (O. E. *léas,* Germ. *los,* cf. *forléosan,* to lose). We find:— C. P. B. 221:—shamlesse;—Areop.: —blamelesse, bottomlesse, fruitlesse, mercilesse, namlesse, uselesse, expencelesse, matchlesse; Anim.:—numberlesse, uselesse; L. to H.:—fearlesse, doubtlesse; but also:—Areop.:—haples, doubtles; L. to H.:—fadomles.

In M. E. this ending appears both as "lēs," and as *les,* with the vowel shortened, which may be due to the influence of *lesse, less;*

4

hence these fluctuations between *lesse* and *les.* The form *less* is not found yet, neither in Milton nor in his contemporaries. Browne (U. B.) has throughout *lesse;* Ex.:—endlesse, fruitlesse, namlesse, restlesse; Herbert too.—We refer also to what we said above concerning the ending *ness* in § 5.

CHAPTER IV.

The Verb.

A. General Remarks.

1. In Early Mn. English the dropping of weak final *e,* together with the M. E. tendency to drop final weak *n,* had a great effect in simplifying the verb inflections. The monosyllabic *bind,* for instance, became the representative of the following M. E. forms:—pres. indic., first person sing. *I binde;* plur. *we binde(n);* pres. subj. *binde, binden.*[1]

In Milton, however, our attention is attracted by a great number of forms in which we find a weak final *e.* Is this *e* to be regarded as a remnant of M. E. verbal inflection, as Rost seems to do, or is it mere phonetic spelling?

 a. Weak final *e* is found in the following verbs ending in a vowel:—
  To doe, which Mätzner mentions as being an orthography peculiar to the XVIIth century (I. 409), and:—to goe, to forgoe (Areop., Ram., C. P. B.).

 b. Verbs ending in *y,* preceded by a consonant, generally appear with the spelling *ie:*—Areop.:—to fortifie, to qualifie, to satisfie; L. to H.:—to trie (twice); Anim., p. 16:—to justifie; Prel. Episc. 1, 2:—to satisfie.

 c. Verbs ending in a consonant:—
  α. Verbs ending in a double consonant (preceded by a short vowel) and bearing the stress on the last syllable:—Ram. 39, to passe (2); 38, to redresse; C. P. B. 181, to incurre;—

---

[1] Sweet. Op. cit. 384.

Areop.:—adde, barre, confesse, dismisse, expresse, passe (5), redresse, suppresse, transgresse, being all of Latin or Norman-French origin;—L. to H.:—adde, deferre, guesse, quaffe, tugge;—Col.:—to adde;—Doct. and Disc. of Div.:—I, erre; II, addresse, dismisse, passe.

β. The following forms, either of monosyllabic verbs, or of such dissyllabic verbs as have the stress on their last syllable:—Ram. 40:—to warne; C. P. B.:—to seale; 181, 182, to governe, to patterne, must then have borne the stress on their last syllable;—Anim. 10:—to seeme, to learne;—Prel. Episc.:—to retaine;—R. of Ch. Gov. Pref.:—to aime, feare, informe, keepe, feare;—Eikon. 6:—to heare;—Areop.:—affirme, finde (spelt throughout *"finde"*, O. E. *findan*), forbeare (O. E. *forberan*), impaire, thinke (O. E. geþencan);—L. to H. and Col.:—to finde;—Col.:—maintaine;—D. and Disc. of Div. I, beare (O. E. *beran*), thinke; II, feele (O. E. *felan*), informe, seeke (O. E. *secean, secan,* M. E. *seken*); III, appeare, performe, thinke; IV, burne (O. E. *brennan, bernan,* M. E. *bernen*), meane (O. E. *maenan,* M. E. *menen*), passe, seeke, thinke; V, dispaire; VI, finde, keepe (O. E. *cepan,* M. E. *kepen*), returne, soile (O. Fr. *souil,* hence *souiller;* cf. O. E. *solian, sylian,* Lat. *foedare;* Goth. *bisouljan*); VII, breake (O. E. *brecan,* M. E. *breken*).

This *e* occurs not only in the infinitive, but also in the conjugation of these verbs, without distinction of mood, or tense, or person. So we find:—pres. indic., indiscriminately, first and third person sing. and plur.;—Areop.:—How Bookes demeane themselves; as they daily expresse their thoughts; those who possesse the imployment; first person, I feare our English will not finde; I finde; second person, ye professe;— preterite:—The first who tooke it up (tooke occurs 3 times);— subj. pres.:—Ere any aske;—imperative:—adde.—L. to H., indic. pres.:—I thinke; you professe; the comedies that treate; where they passe;—past part.:—Ram.:—slaine (frequently throughout); C. P. B. 160, groone; 179, sworne.

2. Other writers have this *e* as well, Bacon, Ad. of L.:—to appeare, to attaine, to bee (2), to cleere, to doe, to drinke, to discerne, to finde

(2), to outcompasse, to reveale, to referre, to sette forth, to speake, to thinke; I heare, they doe (3); if it bee; I thinke; past part., beene, borne, knowne, understoode;—Of the true greatnesse of K. and Estates, Cam. Ser.:—to adde, aime, attaine, appeare, beare, claspe, containe, deale, doe, expresse, faile, gaine, keepe, meane, professe, speake, thinke. Past part., beene, seene:—Herbert, Hist. of Geo.:— to beate, to obtaine, to speake; past part., seene.—

Taylor, α, to aske, to adde, to doe (2), to guesse, to learne, to professe; I confesse, I finde; β, to coole, to goe, to warre; pres. indic., I meane; past part., seene; (a Sermon, Cam. Ser.):—to breake, doe, gaine, meane, passe, performe, professe, speake, thinke; past part., beene.

Hobbes, H. N.:—to finde, to summe, to winne; pres. ind., I erre (3). Of the Liberty of Subjects, Cam. Ser.:—to appeare, doe, inferre, to abhorre, to adde, concurre, conforme, coole, passe, solicite.— Browne, U. B.:—to doe, we finde.

3. This weak final *e* cannot possibly be a verbal inflection, for, if it were one, we should no doubt meet it regularly in certain forms; that is not the case. It occurs exceedingly frequently, but it often fails, too. We are nearest to the truth if we simply explain it as the *"qualifying e"* mentioned in the preceding chapter, and of which we shall have occasion to speak again, when treating the substantive.—Be it as it may, we notice in Milton a distinct tendency (stronger than in his contemporaries) to drop and avoid, in writing, all that could not be scientifically accounted for, as, for instance, this arbitrary means of bringing about an agreement between orthography and so fluctuating a thing as the spoken language.

B. The Inflections.

1. The main innovation, in the Mn. English verb inflections, was the introduction of the Northern *s* in the third person sing., pres. indic. as:—*he calls*.

This introduction took place through the medium of the Midland dialect.

It did however not entirely supplant the older *th* (he calleth), which still survives in the higher literary language.

a. Of that *th* Milton, in opposition to his contemporaries, makes but sparing use. His only prose work in which it is really predominant is his "Accedence Commenc't Grammar," a schoolbook, written in a slightly pedantic style. Here follows a list of the various forms found in it:—agreeth, affordeth, behoveth, betokeneth, biddeth, calleth, cometh, consisteth, declareth, endeth, exceedeth, followeth, formeth, goeth, governeth, hath, irketh, joyneth, maketh, nameth, passeth, requireth (twice), sheweth, signifieth, speaketh, standeth, supplieth.

Three verbs alone form their third person by adding *s*:—governs, occurring twice, requires, signifies (plur.:—they signifie).

b. In his other works and pamphlets Milton uses with great regularity the modern ending *s (es)*, with the exception of the two verbs:—to have and to do, the third person sing. pres. indic. of which mostly occurs as:—"hath, doth"; we occasionally read:—saith (and sayes, saies).

Examples from Ram.:—appeares (4), bewailes, bids, calls, comforts, concludes, dispaires, dyes, gives, instructs, layes, promises, resents, submitts; but:—admonisheth, saith;—C. P. B.:—appeares (2), speakes; but preserveth;—Anim. 10:— sails (2);—Eikon. 1:—laies down; 4, he breakes; 75, he affirmes; 7, he recoiles.

The result of my lecture of the "Letter to Hartlib" has been:—*s* throughout, with one exception:—hath. Areop. gives a like result; exceptions:—hath (32 times; has 6 times), saith (3 times). Doct. and Disc. of Divorce:—similar result; Ex.:—arises, censures, finds, passes, seems, treats.

c. Milton is here taking the lead among his contemporaries, having adopted a uniform spelling and way of forming the third person sing. pres. indic. which stands in perfect agreement with the pronunciation of the day. For, we find in Hodges' "Special help to orthographie," published in 1643, the following indication:—"However wee use to write thus:—*leadeth it, maketh it, noteth it, raketh it, perfumeth it,* &c., yet in our ordinary speech, wee say *leads it, notes it, rakes it, perfumes it.*"[1] And indeed, we find among the examples of "words alike in sound and unlike both in their signification and writing, exprest by

---

[1] Cf. Ellis. Op. cit. IV. 1023.

different letters," the following one:—C.—Cox, a mans sirname. Cocks and Hens. Cocketh up the hay (cf. above p. 16), where *cocketh* must have sounded like *cox* and *cocks.*

2. The weak vowel of the endings *est, eth, es, ed* was dropped in Early Mn. English in the spoken language, except that full *est, es* was always kept after the sibilants (hiss-consonants *s, z*), being subject to exactly the same rules as the noun inflectional *es.* Ex. Milton:— passes, teacheth, teaches, searches; otherwise all these endings were shortened in speech without regard to M. E. forms, as in *heaves, hears.* This fact explains such forms as (Areop.):—behoovs, leavs, meditats, extirpats, resolvs, from the infinitives "leave, resolve." Cf. chapter III. A. 2.

3. *a.* The full ending *es* is generally kept by Milton after the verbs ending in *ay, ey oy, ow,* and *y* preceded by a consonant, the *y* being sometimes kept, sometimes also changed into *i,* even when preceded by a vowel. Ex. Ram. 38, dyes; 40, layes;—C. P. B. 199, lyeth;—Anim. 10, saies (2);—Eikon. 1, laies down;—Areop.:— praies, sayes, slaies; obeyes; destroyes; justifies, lyes;—Col.:— bewraies;—Doct. and Disc. of Div.:—knowes.

b. The same is, of course, the case in the third person of verbs ending in *k, l, m, n, r,* the infinitives of which have kept a qualifying *e.* Ex.:—Ram. 40, appeares (4), bewailes, feares;—C. P. B. 109, 183, appeares; also 58, speakes;—Eikon. 4, breakes; 5, affirmes; 7, re- coiles;—Areop.:—affirmes;—Col.:—performes, soiles, turnes;— D. and Disc. of Div. IV:—remaines, burnes and keepes.

But Milton mostly follows the now adopted rules and writes:— D. and D. of Div. I, II:—stands, hinders, holds; III, runs; IV, brings, diverts, seeks (infin. seeke); VII, disturbs.

4. As an anomaly, we may take note of the inflected third person of the verb *to dare.* Areop.:—"The printer dares not go beyond, &c." Commonly, when we use *dare* (O. E. *durran*) with another verb, we do not inflect the third person; we treat it like the auxiliary verbs; but, when it governs the accusative, then we inflect it. We say:— "he dare not go," but "he dares him to go" (challenges, Greek:— θαῤῥεῖν, θαρσεῖν). Hales explains that the words are different. The auxiliary *dare,* being really an old preterite to O. E. *durran,* does not, as such, take an *s* in the third person. (Hobbes has regularly "no man dare to obey."—Of Lib. of Subj., Cam. Ser.)[1]

5. Before passing on to the preterite, let us see how Milton's contemporaries formed their third person sing. pres. indic.

Bacon kept *th;* we rarely come across a form in *es, s;* two only could be noted in the passages read:—it workes and it seemes.—

In Hobbes *th* by far prevails; the following forms in *s* (*es*) have alone been found: — Hu. Nat.:—it comes forth; Lib. of Subj., Cam. Ser.: — finds, has (once, but "hath" three times), does (once, doth 3 times); Dissol. of a Commonw., Cam. Ser.:—does (3 times), comes, excludes, has, suffocates, wants; but the forms:—doth, commeth (twice), excludeth, hath (6 times), wanteth, are more frequent, as well as many others like:—endangereth, putteth, representeth, setteth, and so on.

Herbert makes a more frequent use of *s, es.* H. of Geo.:—beseeches, joynes, proclaimes, seemes, shewes, turnes, wants.—So Browne:—Rel. Med., Cam. Ser.:—antiquates, reprobates, runnes; U. B.: — antiquates, addes, bids, makes, reveals, stands, seems, sets, puts, weds; forms with *th* alternate sometimes with forms in *s;* we find in the same sentence, U. B.:—trampleth and sets; then also:—hath, carrieth out, observeth. In the sermons of Jeremy Taylor the forms in *s, es* seem to predominate.

C. The Preterite.

1. *Weak verbs.* The preterite ending *ed,* in weak verbs, was rarely written in full; the absence of *e* was mostly marked by an apostrophe:—*seemed, seem'd, seemd.* The first two spellings—*seemed, seem'd*—continued in common use up to the second half of the last century, the full spelling being now preferred. Defoe (1661—1731) writes for instance:—*oppress'd, ow'd, receiv'd, rescu'd* (Seasonable Warning and Caution). Addison, too (1672—1719), in the "Spectator", mentions this tendency to "close in one syllable the termination of the preterperfect tense," as in the words:—*walk'd, arriv'd, drown'd.*—As to this

---

[1] Hales, Areop. 117.

dropping of weak *e* in Milton, we refer to what we said above in our chapter on orthography A, 1, and go on to discuss

2. *The preterite and past participle of strong verbs.*

a. The change of strong to weak verbs, which can be observed in M. E., and which began by the appearance of weak forms everywhere except in the preterite, went on in the transition from M. E. to Mn. E. and in some cases in Mn. E. itself. On the other hand, several weak verbs have been made strong by the analogy of strong verbs, such as *wear, wore, worn* (O. E. *werian, werede*) by the analogy of *swear, swore, sworn.*[1]

Again, beside the levelling of the distinction between pret. sing. and plur., by phonetic changes in weak verbs, by external analogical changes in strong verbs, there took place a further assimilation of the preterite to the preterite participle, assisted by the fact that the plural form of certain verbs contained the vowel of the past participle.—Thus the plural preterite of *write* was *writen* (O. E. pret. *wrát, writun,* past part. *writen).*—So in the XVIth and XVIIth centuries we find the forms:—*driv, smit, rid, ris,* for *drove, smote, rode, rose;* similarly in Early Mn. E. (and in Milton) we find the preterites *bore, broke, spoke* by the side of *bare, brake, spake* (M. E. *bár, brák, spák*).

Now Milton has not dismissed the older forms. Ex. Areop.:— No envious Juno sate cros-leg'd; (obsolete Mn. E. pret. sate, due to the analogy of came, spake, &c.); they writ in an unknown tongue; as well as any that writ before him; though it were Knox that spake it. Anim. 11:—that begun to close; 15, have you sate still. C. P. B. 58:—who spake ill; 183, the Earl bare the sword.

b. The following past participles are found:—Areop.:—he had broke prison; a poem writ by Homer; D. and D. of Div.:—writt (XIV); "writt'n" is used as adjective:—unwritt'n laws); it is not forgot.— D. and D. of Div.:—a marriage which is more broke.

c. This preference for archaic forms can be traced in Milton's contemporaries as well. Bacon is fond of the ending *en;* he has:— becommen, growen, holpen (O. E. *helpe,* perf. *healp,* plur. *hulpon;* past part. *holpen.—Helped* has replaced the old past *holp; holpen* is

---

[1] Sweet. N. E. Grammar, p. 386.

now archaic).—Hobbes has:—gotten (twice), a form now only found in the Bible.—Walton (Old Songs, Cam. Ser.), I sate.—Browne:—past part. forgot.

D. Future and Conditional.

1. Future and conditional are regularly formed in Milton's prose writings, *shall* and *should* being used in the first person, *will* and *would* in the second and third, singular and plural. Ex.:—Col.:—To sequester out of the world will not mend our condition; they would perhaps change melancholy into sanguin.

In interrogative sentences we notice a more frequent use of *shall* and *should,* in the second and third persons, than in present English. Ex.:—Areop.:—Who shall prohibit them? Shall twenty licencers?—Ref. in England:—Who should oppose it?—

2. Milton makes repeated use of the forms *were* and *had* for the conditional of *to be, to have,* though we occasionally, but not frequently, meet the circumscribed forms *should be, would be; should have, would have.* Areop.:—What were vertue but a name?— L. to H.:—He were nothing so much. It were an injury against nature.—Ref. in England. Book II:—Who should oppose it? The Protestants? They were mad. It had been more for the strength, &c... to tell us.—So Hobbes, Lib. of Subj., Cam. Ser.:—They had had an enemy. Yet Areop.:—It would be better done. What would be best advised?—

E. Cases of the contraction of pronouns

with the verbal forms:—*is, was, will,* so frequent in the modern spoken language, can also be found in Milton's prose. He frequently writes *'tis.* Areop.:—you 'l.—Hobbes separates the pronoun from the verb and writes "'t is said."—Walton:—'twas.

F. Negative and Interrogative Forms.

1. *Negative forms.* Negative sentences with the negation not, as well as interrogative sentences whose subject is not an interrogative pronoun (who, which, what. Ex.:—who said it?), and whose verb is not an auxiliary verb, are, according to present use, to be circumscribed by means of the auxiliary verb *to do,* both in present and preterite. The use of the circumscription is very ancient, [1] but *to do* was originally found only in affirmative sentences, as a means to emphasis. In Early Mn. E. there was no established rule for the insertion and omission of *do* and *did*. The spoken language first adopted it in negative sentences, thence it found its way into written English, but did not begin to prevail until the latter part of the XVIIth century. By Pope's time it was well established. [2] Mätzner gives numerous examples taken from Shakespere, from Par. Lost, &c. "I did not see your grace" (Rich. III. 2, 3). "Do you love me?" (Tempest, 3, 1)—and others; but the instances given, derived chiefly from dramatic poetry, only go to prove, if we read them aright, that as we hinted above, the circumscription was but a means adopted to give more force to the denial, to render the question more pressing and emphatical. In reading or declaiming the words mentioned, we should lay all the stress on the auxiliary verb *to do*. "Do you love me?" would come to mean:—"Do you really, or indeed, love me?" Again, "Do you mean to stop any of William's wages?" II. H[y] IV. 5, 2, would mean:—Do you indeed, &c. . . . ? As a matter of fact, the examples given by Mätzner are but exceptions in the authors from whose works they are taken.—The circumscription was not in use in simple negations in Milton's time, in English prose at least; the influence of the spoken language, in which, no doubt, it existed much earlier, did not contrive to make itself felt in written English until the middle of last century.

a. The following numerous instances may clearly show how little Milton cared for the use of the auxiliary verb *to do*. Areop.:—
Present. I stay not. He flatters not. He who fears not. I know not. I touch not. Men who offend not. I deny not. The execution ends not. I refuse not the paines. We have it not. Ye like not now these authors. God uses not to captivat. Assuredly we bring not innocence into the world. What vertue which knows not the utmost that vice promises. Nor boots it to say for these. I name not him (Arezzo) for posterities sake. We esteem not of that obedience. To alter what precisely accords not with the humor. I endure not an instructer.

---

[1] Mätzner II. 57 and ff.

[2] Essay on Criticism, p. 346, &c.

If her waters (Truth's) flow not in a perpetuall progression. I insist not. If we look not wisely into the sun. They are the troublers who neglect and permit not others to unite those peeces. Though we mark not the method of his counsels. He sees not the firm root. Although I dispraise not the defence of just immunities. We care not to keep Truth separated from Truth. No law can permit it that intends not to unlaw itself. God sees not as man sees, chooses not as man chooses.—*Preterite*. There wanted not among them who suggested such a cours. That which Claudius went not through with.—

Imperative:—Suffer not these prohibitions to stand at every place of opportunity.

Colast.:—*Present*. They that finde not. That which hee understands not. Charity commands not the husband to receav his wife. That makes not the marriage void. All this craft avails him not. I mean not to discuss philosophy.—*Preterite:*—Which our opposite knew not.

Accedence Comm. Gr.:—Such as increase not. In things that have not life. Pronouns differ not in construction . . .

L. to H.:—My inclination leads me not to . . . Every nation affords not to . . . I mean not here.

D. and D. of Div.:—Hinders not. VII. Though they understand it not. Who sees not.—*Preterite*. It hinder'd not the Jews.—Eikon. 6:—He doubted not. 10:—Neither want wee examples.—C. P. B. 181:—He shames not to reverse.

b. So Bacon:—Of true greatn., Cam. Ser.:—They enter not upon wars. Those come nearest the Truth that fetch not their reasons, &c.

But:—Some reason which we doe not know.

The following examples of negative sentences are taken from Herbert, Hist. of Geo.: — The best beautie wants not blemishes.— Taylor:—α. Carefull that he offend not in his tongue. God accepts not of anything we give. He denyes not this. We know not what to aske. I know not.—β. I considered not. I knew them not. I knew not how to get farther.—Hobbes, Hu. Nat.:—True knowledge begetteth not doubt. If reasoning aright winne not consent. Truth and the interest of man oppose not each other.—Lib. of Sub., Cam. Ser.:—

We use not to say.—Dissol. of a Commonw.:—They reason not well.
I see not why. I know not. They say not.—Browne, U. B.:—There
wanted not grounds for this. They stickt not to give their bodies
to be burnt. When they burnt not their dead bodies. They con-
formed not unto the Romane practice. Though they embraced not
this practice, yet entertained they many ceremonies.

Rel. Med., Cam. Ser.:—They who understand not the globe of
the Earth. Where naturall logick prevails not. Men disparage not
antiquity. Five languages secured not the epitaph of Gordianus.—
Imperative:—Confound not the distinctions of thy life. Think not, &c.

c. Very few cases are to be found in which the negation is circumscribed. Areop.:—I did not flatter. (He declares with emphasis
that he did not flatter.) If we doe not hold the truth guiltily, which
becomes not, if we condemn not our teaching. We doe not see.
What withholds us that we doe not give them gentle meetings, that
we debate not the matter of these sophisms. I skill not.

By the time Miège wrote his grammar, the circumscription by
means of "to do" had already gained ground. He states it as a rule,
and explains that the negation *not* is to be placed immediately after
the auxiliary verb. (p. 89).

2. *Interrogative sentences* were not treated in a different manner.
Areop.:—Who finds not that Irenæus and others discover more
heresies then they well confute? What wants there to such a soile?
Who knows not that there be of Protestants? What does he therefore?—Colast.:—Follows it therefore that we must not avoid them?
Eikon. 1:—Who knows not?—Herbert (Hist. of Geo.):—What knew
they?

3. We find on the other hand that Milton frequently uses the
verb *to do* in *affirmative sentences,* in order, as we said above, to bring
more force to bear upon his words, as for instance: — It was the task
which I began with: — to shew that no nation did ever use this way
of licencing. Wherefore did he create passions within us. Books are
not absolutely dead things, but doe contain a potencie of life . . .
They do preserve. The chief cause why sects and schisms doe so
much abound. When God did enlarge the universall diet. (Areop.).

G. The form *be*.

We are struck by the great number of cases in which the form *be* (subjunctive) is used in affirmative sentences, in the sense of the present indicative, whereas it is restricted now to cases where the subjunctive, the mood of doubt, is required.

Be, Abbott explains, was used in Anglo-Saxon generally in a future sense.—The Anglo-Saxon verb *to be* was made up of three distinct roots:—1) infinitive *wesan,* 2) *beon,* 3) present:—*eom, is.* When the future began to be formed by means of another auxiliary verb (shall, will), the use of *be* was restricted to the subjunctive. Now there may be some truth in Abbott's further explanation that, since the future and subjunctive are closely connected in meaning,—the subjunctive being the mood of uncertainty, doubt, and the future containing, or at least not excluding an idea of doubt as to the possibility of the fulfilment or of the non-fulfilment of the action expressed by the verb (this, I suppose, is the meaning of Abbott's words) —, *bé* came to assume an exclusively subjunctive use, and from the mere force of association came to be used without having the full force of the subjunctive; "so, as a rule, it will be found that *be* is used with some notion of doubt, question, thought, for instance in questions and after verbs of thinking. ('Be my horses ready?' Shakespere, Lear, I, 5, 35)."[1]

He says further:—"Be is also used to refer to a number of persons, considered not individually, but as a kind or class. Hamlet, III, 2, 32:—O, there be players, that I have seen play. Tempest, III, 1, 1:—There be some sports are painful."[2]

Milton makes exactly the same use of *be.* Areop.:—These they be which will bear chief sway in such matters. Many there be that complain of Divine Providence. There be also books which are partly usefull and partly culpable. Another sort there be. There be delights, there be recreations. The shop of warre hath not there more anvils . . . then there be pens and heads there.

---

[1] Abbott. Shakespearian Grammar, §§ 298, 299.

[2] Abbott. Shakespearian Grammar, § 300.

But Abbott's statement does not exactly give an explanation for the use of *be* in these sentences. Morris, on the other hand, simply states that "the root *be* was conjugated in the present tense singular and plural, indicative, as late as Milton's time (cf. Genesis, 43, 2:—We be twelve brethren. Milton, Par. Lost:—If thou beest he. I. 84)."[1]—Surely we may ask why it was so, in certain cases, and not throughout, after *there, this, these?* (cf. There is no book that is acceptable unlesse at certain seasons. Milton, Ar.).

Our opinion is that here the Latin syntax made its influence felt, and that we have not to deal with an abnormal use of a form which was generally recognised as being the subjunctive form. We must remember that the Latin writers made an excessively frequent use of the subjunctive. Now, in the Latin subjunctive mood, both optative and subjunctive have been united to form *one subjective mood;* thus there lies in it the notion of willing, as well as the notion of a mere wishing a doubtful event to take place, or an uncertain state of things to become certain. Its original meaning, however, gradually weakened down to be merely potential, and the subjunctive came to possess the faculty of expressing a supposition, or a more or less definite assertion relating to the possible occurrence of an event.

Now take Milton's sentences, place them in the light of this original meaning of the subjunctive (so often attributed to it by Latin writers), and you will undoubtedly find that here again we have to deal with the influence of Latin syntax.—That is indeed a syntactical question which might be discussed in a special paper devoted to the study of Milton's prose, compared with that of Hooker, Bacon, Hobbes, with a view to bring out its affinities with the Latin syntax.

If we attempted to explain the few examples given above, we might say that, in the first sentence, there is a distinct apprehension, or doubt, or hope expressed as to what will "mend the condition of the English nation." Milton's meaning is this:—Not the licencing of books will do it, but the unwritten laws of vertuous education; these, I hope, I esteem, will bear chief sway, &c. .... The second instance is easily explained too:—"Many there be that complain of Divine Providence. Foolish tongues!" It is but an ellipsis, a figure of

<hr/>

[1] Morris. Outlines of E. Accidence, p. 182.

frequent occurrence in Latin literature. We may supply:—"They say that there be,"or "It is said," "I have heard," "I know." It is a subordinate clause. Supply but the principal clause and the subjunctive is explained.

The third example:—"There be books which are partly usefull and partly culpable," may be explained thus:—"Suppose there be (let there be... sint libri), &c.;" then, this work (of licencing) will require more officials.—I have noted the following two examples from Hobbes:—"There be also that think there may be more soules than one, in a Commonwealth; where men reign that be subject to diversity of opinions, it cannot be so." (Diss. of a Commonw., Cam. Ser.); but:—"There is written on the Turrets of the city of Luca;" "There is a sixth doctrine," &c. (Lib. of Subj., Cam. Ser.).—Milton, Ar.:—"There is no book that is acceptable unlesse, &c."

H. Agreement.

We have already passed beyond the limits of "Accidence," and may perhaps be allowed to add one or two words on the syntactical question of concord.

1. After a collective word, "clergy, nation, state," Milton puts the verb in the plural. Ex. Ram. 41:—"The kindred of Amireo who scape him and conspire against him." "As our obdurate clergy have demeaned the matter." (Ar.) [1]

2. There is no incongruity in that, from our modern point of view, but there is one when Milton leaves the verb in the singular, though it has two subjects connected by "and," making it agree with the second subject. Areop.:—Our faith and knowledge thrives by exercise. The blaze that Zuinglius and Calvin hath beaconed up to us. Where one mind and person pleases aptly. The Rabbins and Mamonides tells us. Both love and peace, both nature and religion mourns to be separated. Again:—Unlesse he be a thing heroycally vertuous, and that are not the common lump of men ("the common lump of men" being subject). Doct. and Disc. of Div. II, IV, V, VI.

---

[1] Cf. Jörss, Paul. Grammatisches und Stilistisches aus Milton's Areopagitica. Ratzeburg. 1893. pp. 9, 10.

3. Bacon offers an interesting instance of a collective word "nation," followed by the verb in the singular "doth," but the object is accompanied by the possessive adjective "their":—"No nation which doth not directly professe armes, may looke to have greatnesse fall into their mouths." (Of true greatnesse, &c., Cam. Ser.).—Taylor, β:—Halfe my thoughts was fixt upon the present concernments.—Browne, Rel. Med., Cam. Ser.:—Whilst the mercies of God doth promise us heaven. U. B.:— Misery make Alcmenas nights. A great part of antiquity contented their hopes with a transmigration of their souls.—Civill society carrieth out their dead, and hath exequies.

From these examples we can see that the rules of concord or agreement between verb and subject were still very unsettled.

CHAPTER V.

The Substantive.

By the beginning of the Mn. E. period, the substantives had already been so far modified in their inflection as to keep but the *s* of the Saxon genitive, as well as *s*, mark of the plural. If, then, a number of substantives occur which are spelt with a weak final *e*, where according to present use we should not expect one, this *e* is no doubt the sign of length which we have discussed in the preceding chapters.

A.

1. This qualifying *e* is to be found chiefly after monosyllabic nouns containing a long root-vowel, then also after dissyllabic nouns bearing the stress on the second (last) syllable, whenever those nouns end in the sibilant *s, ss,* in *l, m, n, r,* in *nd, f.*—In many cases, however, Milton's spelling does not differ from the present. and double forms are frequently met.—Words ending in *ss* generally take the *e*. Ex. C. P. B. 58:—crosse; 185, successe Anim.:—presse, trespasse.—

Areop.:—accesse, adresse, blisse, crosse, glasse, losse (4), presse (throughout spelt thus), progresse, successe.—Col.:—buzze.—L. to H.:—amisse.—Doct. and Disc. of Div.:—losse.

Ram. 40:—feare; 37, warre, starre.—C. P. B. 109:—yeares; 186, 243, warre; 221, the answere, feare.—Areop.:—backdore, feare, warre, yeare (year).—Doct. and Disc. of Div.:—dispaire, but constantly:—warre.

Ram. 37:—plaine, reigne; 40, dreames, ruine.—C. P. B. 182:—crowne; 221, reigne, summes; 199, soveraigne; 242, custome.—Areop.:—esteeme, forme, realme, designe, latine, straine.—Col.:—ramme, designe.

Ram. 37:—the monke; 40, the golden calfe, greife.—C. P. B. 17:—healthe; 58, the booke; 182, sporte, tombe; 221, the seale (3); 242, spoile.—Areop.:—soule, soile, booke, kinde, rinde, stuffe, whiffe. —Col.:—taile, minde (throughout).—L. to H.:—halfe, stuffe; kinde, mankinde, minde (2).—Doct. and Disc. of Div.:—griefe, soule (O. E. *sáwol*).—Of Norman-French origin is:—oyle (M. E. *oile, oyle;* O. Fr. *oille, ole;* Mod. Fr. *huile).*

2. That Milton spelt the words ending in *at(e)* throughout without *e,* as a sign of the shortness of the ending, has been stated above, in our chapter on spelling. Ex.:— magistrat, plur. magistrats; palat; tractat, plur. tractats; prelat, plur. prelats; apostat; dictat.

"Tast" and "hast" are spelt as they were in M. E. *" Tast"* is the Old French form, as well, whereas "hast" was O. Fr. *"haste."*—In "vertu" (spelt also vertue) we meet the M. E. and O. Fr. form *vertu.*

3. If here again we compare Milton with Bacon and other contemporaries, we find perfect agreement. "Qualifying *e"* is found at the end of similar words, not only in the nominative, but also in the genitive, dative and accusative. Ex. Bacon, Ad. of L.:—glasse; eare (2), feare (plur. feares); atheisme, fourme, summe, venome; crowne, fountaine, patterne, sinne; sparke, worke, minde (8), the proude, seede, soule, zeale, St. Paule, a thinge; fruite.—Of true greatn., Cam. Ser.:—asse (nom.), compasse; doore, metaphore (pr. metaphóre), warre (nom., gen., acc.); arme, custome, stemme; sunne, crowne, graine, swaine, Spaine.—Henry VII., Cam. Ser.:—chamberlaine, Earle of

5

Lincolne; battaile, soile, weale, behalfe, mischiefe, wolfe; bulke, the darke, workemen; the sheepe, whelpe.

Herbert, Hist. of Geo.:—baptisme, heathenisme; crowne (2), the moone, towne; sonne (4); travaile, battaile (4), combate; beliefe.

Taylor, α:—successe, forme (3); designe, fountaine.—β:—successe, the aire, warre.

Hobbes, Lib. of Sub., Cam. Ser.:—feare, chaine, plur. chains, Romanes (once Romans).—Diss. of C., Cam. Ser.: —warre (throughout), schoole, soule; forme, in summe, venime and venome; sinne; dogge (the *o* being open but lengthened).—Hu. Nat.:—harme, the summe; a signe, in Latine; the aire (and air); mankinde.

Browne, U. B.:—the crosse; the warre; bottome, custome; urne (2), the runne; mankinde, kinde, winde and sword.—Rel. Med., Cam. Ser.:—groane, tooke, little flocke; feete.—U. B., Cam. Ser.: —the kisse, balsame (plur. balsoms), bottome; mountaine, urne, sunne; the dogge starre; the winde (*i* being pronounced like *i* in blind, a pronunciation now restricted to poetry); the houre.

B. The Gender of Substantives.

Milton writes as a rule in accordance with the modern views as to the gender of substantives. Individuals belonging to the male sex are masculine; individuals belonging to the female sex are feminine; things without life, not being of either sex, are neuter.

He differs, however, in the treatment of abstract words. The frequent cases in which they are personified betray the poet.[1]

"*Mind*" in Doct. and Disc. of Div. is often personified, and is spoken of as though it were a male being. Ex. Cap. III:—"The mind shall be thought good enough, and must serve, though to the eternall disturbance of him that complains him."—So in the autogr. letter, Trinity Coll. MS., p. 6, *Mind*:—to declare *herself*.

The earth, countries and cities, night, darkness, the arts and sciences, abstract conceptions as nature, liberty, charity, mercy,

[1] Cf. Gottschalk. Ueber den Gebrauch des Artikels in Milton's Par. Lost. Leipzig. 1892.

religion, the soul, the gentler emotions, are spoken of, in our days, as though they were female beings; so does Milton treat them, cf. the list given by Jörss in his dissertation on "Areopagitica," p. 1.— To this I add the following instances found in Doct. and Disc. of Div.:— "Truth" is feminine, in Cap. I, II, &c.; "Love" in one and the same sentence is both masculine and feminine, Cap. VI:—"Love, if *he* be not twin born, yet hath a brother wondrous like *him,* called Anteros:— whom, while *he* seeks all about his chance is to meet with many false and faining desires, that wander singly up and down in *her* likeness."— In the same chapter "Human contemplation" is feminine:—"One of the highest arks that human contemplation circling upwards, can make from the globy sea whereon she stands."—In Areop. "Reason," though personified and spelt with a capital letter, is neuter:—"He kills Reason itselfe."—Eikon. 2:—the House (of Parliament) and her worthiest members.

C. The Plural of Substantives.

1. The formation of the plural, by means of the ending *s (es),* is carried on regularly in Milton and does not differ from the present mode, except in very few cases.

a. Words ending in a consonant, monosyllabic for the best part, to which Milton adds, as we have seen above, a phonetic *e* to denote length of root-vowel, of course have in the plural *es,* and not *s* merely.— So C. P. B.:—900 yeares;—Areop.:—armes, bookes (and books), chaplaines (and chaplains), dores, Gothes, mindes, paines, starres, windes, workes;—Colast.:—dores, heires, Jewes, mindes;—L. to H.:— aphorismes, (but maxims), designes, lawes, meanes, mindes, mouthes, play-writes (play-wrights);—Doct. and Disc. of Div., I:—kingdomes; VI, breades; VII, teares, maximes;—Eikon. 1, 5:—affaires; 5, the sparkes.

b. In present English we form the plural of nouns ending in *y,* preceded by a vowel, by the mere addition of *s.* Yet Milton regularly writes:—dayes, daies, boyes, wayes, waies, keyes, (but journeys). ("The glorious waies of truth, many waies." Areop.)—Doct. and

Disc. of Div.:—Sundayes, rayes.. Now these words ending in *y* are instances of the solution of an Anglo-Saxon consonant *g, ʒ,* into a vowel *i, ie,* and in them the ending *e* of the nominative and accusative of the weak masculine and neuter nouns (like:—nom., acc., dat. *eie,* plur. *eien)* seems to have survived till very late; indeed the singular forms *daie, weie, waie* occur in the writings of Milton and of his contemporaries, and thus an explanation is given for the plurals "wayes, dayes, keyes," &c. - They can hardly be regarded as consequences of the unsettled spelling *y* for *ie,* to which we referred above (p. 34).

2. Bacon, too, writes in accordance with his phonetic spelling. Ad. of L.:—actes (2), fountaines (2), lawes, partes, shewes (of learning), thinges (2), wordes, workes (2) and works, yeeres; affaires, armes, aides, battailes, boughes, customes, ensignes, farmes, graines, kingdomes, lawes, meanes, the oddes, plaines, sinewes, sonnes, spoiles, townes, triumphes, yeeres;—Hy. VII, Cam. Ser.:—blowes, othes, tearmes, workes.— Herbert, Hist. of Geo.:—arrowes, armes, customes, feares (2), heires, joyes, lawes, the newes, showres, sighes, sorrowes, soules, Turkes (5), troupes, yeeres, tavernes.—Jeremy Taylor, Cam. Ser.:—lawes, meanes, soules, schooles, veynes;—α:—the lawes, meanes; β:—aides, meanes.

Browne, Rel. Med., Cam. Ser.:—swarmes, rankes;—U. B.: — designes, emblemes (pr. emblēmes), epithetes (pr. epithḗtes), mountaines, urnes;—memento's with elided *e* and apostrophe, just like Milton:—Arcadia's, &c. (cf. Jörss, p. 1).

Hobbes, Hu. Nat.:— 2 kindes, lawes; he has throughout:— lawes;—Dissol. of a Com., Cam. Ser.:—armes, designes, kingdomes, lawes, limbes, soules, summes, warres, wormes.

These writers also form the plural of *way* and *day* like Milton.— Bacon has throughout:—waies, alwayes;—Hobbes:—wayes;— Walton:—dayes;—Browne, U. B.:—waies, wayes (2), dayes (3); Herbert. Hist. of Geo.:—dayes, wayes;—Taylor, β:—wayes.

3. *Army* is used as a collective word in:—the Army of thir own accord being beat'n in the north. (Eikon. 4.) So *youth* in Ram. 39:—They send two of thire choysest youth. So Anim. 11:—The 1000 *Horse. Meanes* is singular:—Anim. 2:—by this meanes (2).

D. The Possessive Case

alone has retained an inflectional ending:—the suffix *es, s,* which originally belonged to the genitive singular of some masculine and neuter substantives, and, in the XIIIth century only, became the genitive sign of the feminine gender as well.

1. The use of this "Saxon" genitive, in Milton, is hardly ever extended to things, but is restricted to the names of living beings:— the following cases have been found in Ram. 38:—Adams ruine; the Danes negligence; Alfreds reigne; Edward Confessors divorsing and imprisoning his noble wife Editha, Godwins daughter; 39, Abrahams strange voiage; thire mistresse sorrow; her daughters dancing; his wives daughter; thire maisters return; 40, in thire maisters defence; Lots journey; at the priests inviting; Adams fall.—C. P. B. 74:—His wives pride; 109, the Popes legates; 160, the peoples disposition; 179, lawyers opinions; the Londoners request; the Popes curse; 220, his subjects love; every mans goods.—Areop.:—In Gods esteeme; every mans copy; the Dragons teeth; Gods image; leaving it to each ones conscience; over mens eyes; from the West End of Pauls; any mans intellectual offspring; each mans discretion; the diet of mans body; every mans daily portion; St. Pauls converts; mans life; these are the country-mens Arcadia's; his censors hand; a coits distance; learned mens discouragement; the peoples birthright; Hercules Pillars; her masters second comming; all the Lords people; for honours sake; Gods ordinances; the Angels ministery; Gods enlightning his church; the printers and the authors name, or at least the printers; mans prevention; other mens vassalls; two hours meditation.—Anim. 5:—The Devils name.—Prel. Episc.:—For truths sake.—Eikon. 1:—By others advice; 3, of one Naboths vineyard; the peoples interest; 5, the kings affaires; 7, his childrens interest; some mens rigour of remisseness; 8, the peoples hatred; 10, the Archbishops late Breviary.—The letter to Hartlib contains these instances:— Gods working; Aristotles poetics; Senecas naturall questions.— Colast.:—A mans heart; by the licencers law; som knights chaplainship; a drones nest; other mens miseries.—Doct. and Disc. of Div.:— Mans nature; Cap. I, our Saviours words; Natures impression; mans

life; Cap. II, his neighbors bed; Natures working; VI, Loves sphere; his mothers own sons; Solomons advice; for loves sake; VII, a Christian mans life; Gods providence; mans iniquitie.

From these examples it is evident that in Milton's time the vowel *e* of the ending had already been dropped. The few exceptions which have been found shall be mentioned below.

2. The loss of the final vowel *e* is indicated in Present English by the *apostrophe* ('), which was at first probably used to distinguish the genitive from the plural suffix. Milton does not use this sign yet, although, as we have seen, he rarely fails to denote the elision of a weak vowel in the body or in the ending of a word, — as in the past participle endings *ed, en*.—In the whole pamphlet "Areopagitica" there is only one instance of an apostrophe used in the Saxon genitive of a proper name ending in a vowel:—Plato's licencing of books (cf. above, the plurals:—Arcadia's, Balcone's).—Doct. and Disc. of Div.:—Beza's opinion. (Cap. XIV.)

3. Words ending in *y*, preceded by a consonant, change *y* into *ie* before *s*, just as we are wont to do now, when the plural ending *s* must be added to them; but this is perhaps a consequence of Milton's rule not to use the apostrophe. Thus we have:—L. to H.:—For memories sake.—Areop.:—Their countries liberty; for posterities sake.—Doct. and Disc. of Div.:—The bodies delight.

4. The general use of the *apostrophe* in the singular is not found much before the end of the XVIIth century. It was at first intended only to show contraction of *es*, and was accordingly freely used in the plural as well as the genitive inflection. The gradual restriction of the apostrophe to the genitive apparently arose from the belief that such a genitive as *prince's*, in *the prince's house*, was a shortening of *prince his*, as shown by such spellings for the genitive as *the prince his house*. It was indeed a peculiar idiom, as late as Johnson's and Addison's time, to use a demonstrative pronoun to mark the grammatical relation (of possession chiefly) of some other word or group of words; but it seems to have been restricted to cases in which relation to persons had to be expressed. Bacon has for instance:— Cicero writing of Pompey his preparation against Cæsar.—Yet Herbert,

Hist. of Geo.:—The fairest day its showres.—Jeremy Taylor:—
Oure deare Master his royal lawes.—Browne (Rel. Med.):—Phalaris
his Bull; (U. B.):—Moses his man.—This belief, and this spelling,
arose very naturally from the fact that *prince's* and *prince his* had the
same sound, weak *his* having dropped its *h* in such collocations, even
in the O. E. period.[1]

Butler (Grammar, p. 35) clearly attributes the genitive ending *s*
to a shortening of *his,* and explains "my masters son," as being the
contraction of:—my master his son.—Hodges (Primrose) tells us
that:—"The apostrophus or mark of contraction, is the same with
the comma, ônely the difference is of place; for, this stands not in
the line, but over the upper part thëreof, where the contraction is:—
and it is most commonly ûs'd, when two words come together, th' ône
ending in a vowel, and th' other beginning with a vowel:—for then
such two words may bee contracted by taking away the vowel in the
first, as in these words:—*th' Apostles* for *the Apostles; th' intent* for *the
intent;* or else when a word of two syllables by contraction is made
ône, as *sav'd* for *saved, liv'd* for *lived, lov'd* for *loved,* &c. But in this
work I make but little use of an apostrophus in such as the latter
words aforegoing:—I rather use a silent *e* in stead there of, as, not
sav'd, liv'd, and *lov'd,* but *saved, lived, loved."*

Not the slightest allusion is made to the dropping of the genitive *e,* nor to its being replaced by an apostrophe.

Miège (p. 66) gives a careful explanation of the genitive ending
s, es, and distinctly mentions the introduction of an apostrophe:—
"Remarquez qu'ici on ajoute une apostrophe et une *s. My father's
house, my mother's estate.* C'est ce qu'il faut observer lorsque la chose
exprime possession." He goes on to say that this *s* is frequently
regarded as a contraction of *"his,"* because that pronoun is occasionally made use of in the formation of the genitive, as in:—*Peter his
house.* It is, however, an entirely false notion, for:—*A Virgin's beauty*
cannot possibly stand for:—*A Virgin his beauty,* Virgin being feminine.[2]
"L'apostrophe est donc plutôt une distinction de nombres. Sans laquelle

---

[1] Cf. Sievers. A.-S. Grammar, § 217 and "Anmerkung 1."
[2] Milton writes (Bi. Ms.):—My wife his mother.

le substantif étant revêtu d'une *s*, au singulier, préviendrait d'abord l'esprit d'une fausse idée en lui faisant paraître ce nom là au pluriel."— He finds, however, this apostrophe superfluous in words whose plural does not end in *s*, and those "qui entendent bien cette matière," do not add it. So he would write:—*a womans beauty.* The use of the apostrophe is what he calls a "délicatesse" of the English language, based on reason, and established (établie) by custom. He too, sensible as he is, fails to recognize the true nature of *s (es)*.

In the gen. plur. Miège drops, not the second, but the first of the two *s*. So he writes:—*the souldier's arms,* as in the singular, for:— the arms of the souldiers. Milton too, writes, as we have seen above:— The Danes negligence; lawyers opinions; the Londoners request; his subjects love; by others advice.

Gill (p. 75, Logon.), discussing the "Substantiva casus regentia," mentions the *"genitive of possession,"* formed by adding a soft *s--ȝ*, without apostrophe. Ex.:—*A friends business:—a frindȝ biȝnes.*

5. The formation of the Saxon genitive by means of *s* was, however, the regular one. Bacon:—A mans body; mens armes; the lions whelpe; mens courage; gentlemans labourer;—Adv. of L.:—your majesties employments; of anothers knowledge; your majesties manner; natures order; since Christs time; other mens wits; mans enquirie; Gods creatures.—Herbert, Hist. of Geo.:—Regarding his owne great yeares and sonnes (his omitted the second time) deservings; their owne ambition and others assassinations; other mens minds; the nights darknesse; in that days combate; the generals tent; the kings tent; (note:—Sicala's sonne; gifts unworthy such a master).—Taylor, too, has:—Mens resolutions; any mans religion; the popes subject;—α:—Gods vouchsafeing; Solomons reason; Gods spirit; Christs ascension;—β:—Mens interests; Gods disposition; Gods mercy.—Hobbes, Lib. of Sub., Cam. Ser.:—Mans will; mans actions; Gods will; Gods subject;—Diss. of Comm., Cam. Ser.:—A mans conscience; mens mindes; mans nature; the soveraigns right; Your Lordships favour; the authors advice.—Browne, U. B.:— Hippocrates patients; Achilles horses; each others will; one anothers salvation.

6. The following genitives may also be noticed:—the daies work (L. to H.), and:—the soules contentment; genitive of soule (Doct. and Disc. of Div.). — Bi.:—Wedén'sday (1648), being Wodan's day. Finally the genitive of wife is:—wive's, with change of *f* into *ve,* just as in the plural. Cf. above:—his wives daughter, his wives pride.

The influence of E. E. may perhaps be traced in the form:— thire mistresse sorrow (Ram., p. 39). The suffix *es,* as already stated, originally belonged to the genitive singular of masculine and neuter substantives only. It was not the genitive sign of the feminine until the XIIIth century, and then for the most part only in the northern dialect. Cf. Morris, Accid., p. 101.— Or is its explanation to be sought in the pronunciation of the word "mistresse"?

7. In stating the relationship of one person to another, we use to-day the genitive case; Milton still used the preposition *to,* after the proper name:—Ram. 37:—Ewin, son to Edward the yonger; Venutius, husband to Cartismandua; 38, Gunilda, daughter to Hard Canute; Emma, wife to Henry the third; and in C. P. B. 179:— afterwards being prisoner to the Barons.

CHAPTER VI.

The Adjective.

A. General Remarks.

1. In early Mn. English the loss of final *e* made the adjectives indeclinable, as far as case and number are concerned. Adjectives thus became formally indistinguishable from adverbs, except by their syntactical relations, the only change of form that was left to them, namely comparison, being shared by adverbs.

a. And yet in Milton's prose we meet a small number of adjectives, ending in a consonant, to which is added a weak final *e,* without regard to the form (whether definite or indefinite), nor to case. Such adjectives may be of German or of French origin, indifferently, but they are chiefly monosyllabic, or, if polysyllabic, they bear the

principal stress on their last syllable; and this characteristic they have
in common, that their root vowel is long.—The following instances
were found in C. P. B. 179:—faire; 199, firme.—Areop.:—certaine,
foreine, forreigne, meane, mine, modérne, owne, plaine; firme, deare,
milde; publicke, weake, steepe.—Doct. and Disc. of Div.:—owne,
solémne, vaine (and vain), farre.—L. to H.:—meere, farre; briefe,
chiefe, deafe; odde.—Areop.:—grosse, remisse.—Anim.:—humane,
owne, uncertaine.—Eikon. 9:—faire.—R. of Ch. Gov.:—humane,
vaine.

But this spelling was not by any means settled, for, although
these adjectives may occur repeatedly being spelt with *e,* yet the
number of cases in which the *e* is dropped is quite as great. Ex.
Areop.:—"They wounded us with our own weapons, and with our
owne arts;" "vaine" and "vain."—This *e* must however have a meaning, and the most natural explanation that can be given for it, is to
regard it as a phonetic sign (of the length of the preceding vowel);
we can but refer to what we said above, when discussing the qualifying *e* in our chapters on spelling, the verb, and the substantive.

b. If we compare Milton with other writers of the period, we
cannot help being struck by the strong tendency he shows to drop
that *e,* which disappears in Eikon., while Bacon and others still use
it with great regularity. Ex. from Bacon:—Adv. of L.:—certaine,
civile, humane (2), owne (2), prophane, soveraigne, vaine; extreame,
supreame; solide, weake; cleane, firme, owne, suddaine, weake.—
Herbert:—plaine, deere; owne (4), solemne, uncertaine.—Taylor,
α:—certaine, humane, maine, owne (2), publike (4); β:—coole,
humane (2), publike (3); (own without e); halfe; deare, owne.—
Hobbes:—firme, westerne, latine;—Hu. Nat.:—lucide (5).—Browne,
U. B.:—owne, the Romane practice (2); blinde, briefe, halfe, mine,
straite, vaine, wilde.—The French form may have influenced Milton
in spelling:—moderne.

c. At the end of a short syllable weak final *e* is frequently
omitted, even where modern orthography requires it. Ex.:—wors
(throughout with very rare exceptions), of German origin;—M. E. *wors;*
O. E. *wyrs.* So also in adjectives formed by means of the suffix *some;*
O. E. *sum:*—troublesom, wearisom (and wearisome).—Lastly in ad-

jectives of Romance origin with the suffix *ate, ile, ine.* Arcop.:—
privat, compassionat, considerat, consummat, elaborat, moderat, obdurat, obstinat; sanguin; fragil, facil.—French influence may have
made itself felt in *divers,* (so Bacon, throughout:—divers).

2. *a.* Another feature of interest in Milton is the regular doubling of the final consonant *l* in adjectives. I think there lies in it
more than a mere peculiarity of phonetic spelling, such as the one
discussed in chapter III, A, 1, for it is carried through with great
regularity in the writers of the period, and may certainly be traced
far back. A quotation from ten Brink, "Chaucer's Sprache und Vers-
kunst," § 96 et seq., may perhaps throw some light on the subject.
He says, § 97: — "Schon in A. E. Zeit galt die Regel, dass ursprünglich
kurze Konsonanz im Auslaut einer betonten Silbe gedehnt wurde.
Hierauf beruht ein grosser Teil der Erscheinungen, die im gewöhn-
lichen Sprachgebrauch unter dem Namen Position zusammengefasst
werden. Auf diese Weise wurden viele ursprünglich kurze Silben lang,
ursprünglich lange Silben überlang, ein Uebermass, dessen sich die
Sprache dann im Laufe der Zeit durch Vokalkürzung zu entledigen
suchte. Diese Konsonantendehnung trat aber nicht ein, wenn der
Silbenauslaut mit dem Wortauslaut zusammenfiel, daher konnten
kurze konsonantisch auslautende Monosyllaben im A. E. nur unter
dem Versictus für lang gelten. In M. E. Zeit aber wirkte der *Satzton
mit der Intensität des Ictus,* daher alle kurzen Konsonanten im Wortauslaut nach betontem kurzem Vokal gedehnt wurden."—Now we
find that in M. E. the French suffix *al* (animal, celestial), for instance,
constantly rimes with *all* (shall, small) and bears a strong secondary
stress.[1]

This stress it still distinctly bore, in prose and verse, in Milton's
time:[2] thus may be explained the regular occurrence of the forms in

[1] The following instances have been found in the first book of *Spenser's*
" *Fairy Queen,*" I, 8:—all rimes with funerall; II, 20, fall—funerall; 36, martiall—
call; III, 16, call— severall—criminall; V, 22, all—cœlestiall—hall; 53. stall—
funerall—fall; VI, 26, compell—cruell—fell; VIII, 1, continuall—thrall; X, 34,
all—liberall—fall; 36, hospitall—fall; XI, 22, ill—nosethrill.

[2] In the miscellaneous poems:— *The Hymn,* 15, "hall" rimes with "festivall."
Again, in *An epitaph on the marchioness of Winchester,* we find the following
two verses:

> "Which the sad morn had let fall"
> "On her hastning funerall."

all, ell, ill, found in Ramb.:—aereall, continuall, heroicall, severall.—
C. P. B.:—naturall, cruell.—Areop.:—actuall, artificiall, carnall,
collaterall, elementall, equall, in generall, immortall, incidentall, intellectuall, liberall, manuall, mortall, municipall, natural, national
and nationall, partiall, perpetuall, practicall, principall, reall,
royall, textuall, triviall, unequall, universall.—L. to H.:—effectuall,
equall, incidentall, finall, frugall, generall, legall, liberall, martiall,
morall, naturall, personall, prodigall, rationall, reall, rurall, severall,
speciall, usuall.—Doct. and Disc. of Div., Introd.:—conjugall, mutuall,
naturall; Cap. I, morall, reall; II, carnall, continuall, generall, morall,
perpetuall, principall; III, eternall, irrationall, sensuall, usuall; IV,
formall, originall; VI, generall, liberall, originall; VII, bestiall,
generall.—Areop.:—civill, evill (and evil); O. E. *yfel, ufel, evel, ivel,
ill,* contraction of evil, may have influenced the spelling; untill (O. E.
til; M. E. *till),* scurrill, civill.—L. to H.:—evill, civill.—Doct. and
Disc. of Div.:—cruell, parallell.— This doubling of the final consonant
has thus a twofold meaning. It first indicates that the preceding
vowel was short (cf. III, A, 1), and secondly that the ending bore a
secondary stress.—Withall, also is to be noticed.

b. This spelling is carried through with great regularity by Milton's
contemporaries. Bacon has:—Adv. of L.:—immortall, individuall (2),
intellectuall (2), memoriall, originall (2), principall, substantiall, super-
ficiall, temporall, universall (2); but once "material things."—Herbert,
Hist. of Geo.:—equall (2) and equal (1), generall (2), immortall, unnatu-
rall; cruell.—Taylor, α:—carnall, eternall, finall, naturall (2), severall;
β, collaterall, ineffectuall (4), materiall, mutuall (2), perpetuall, severall,
blood royall; charnell; civill.—Browne, U. B.: — aethereall, animall,
carnall, centrall, corporall, equall (2), finall, formall, funerall (2) pyre,
immortall, integrall, originall, phantasticall, rationall (2), sepulchrall
(2), severall, speciall, totall, urnall; civill (but natural [1]); — Rel.
Med., Cam. Ser.:—equall, mechanicall, mortall, immortall, poeticall,
provinciall, plurall; evill, subtill; cruell.

Hobbes, however, has as a rule *al; all* is an exception.— Hu. Nat.:—
corporeal, dogmatical, equal, general, internal (2), mathematical,
mutual, natural (and naturall), phantastical, principal (2), real, several
(4). But "all," the adjective, occurs regularly.

3. *a.* *Full* combined with nouns to form adjectives takes but one *l* in modern English. Milton, however, in conformity with ancient use, writes *ll*. Ex. Ram. 37:—slothfull; 39, frightfull; 40, dreadfull.—C. P. B. 16:—lawfull; 160, dreadfull; 185, ingratfull.—Areop.:—carefull, cheerfull, disgracefull, delightfull, doubtfull, faithfull, hurtfull, lawfull, painfull, skilfull, sportfull, unlawfull, usefull. —L. to H.:— artfull, delightfull, gracefull, healthfull, helpfull, youthfull, needfull, skillfull, unsuccessfull, usefull.—Doct. and Disc. of Div. I:—lawfull, usefull; III, carefull, cheerfull, lawfull; IV, cheerfull (cheerefull); VI, blisfull, needfull.—Eikon.:—mindfull.

b. Bacon has regularly:—Adv. of L.:—joyfull, fearefull, gracefull, healthfull.—Herbert, Hist. of Geo.:—faithfull, usefull.—Taylor, α:—lawfull, carefull; β, mercifull, unusefull.—Hobbes, Cam. Ser.:— delightfull, lawfull, painfull. — Browne, U. B.:—lawfull, mercifull, mournfull.

4. Milton frequently substantifies adjectives, and follows in the main the rules now in force. In the following instance, however, he has omitted the indefinite pronoun *one,* which adjectives generally require when used substantively, in the singular.—Anim. 8:—the wiser in many points. — But Areop.:—The labours of the dead.

5. This carelessness in the adding of *one* is more frequent when, two adjectives being related to one substantive, and the latter being placed immediately after the first of the two adjectives, the second would require the addition of the indefinite pronoun, which becomes itself a substantive, and as such may take the mark of the plural. This again belongs to those peculiarities of Milton's style which must be attributed to the influence of the Latin tongue. Ex. Areop.:—That vertue is but a blank vertue, not a pure. Had any one divulged erroneous things and scandalous to honest life; (modern prose grammar would require either "scandalous ones," or rather "things erroneous and scandalous to honest life"). If it be desir'd to know the cause, there cannot be assigned a truer then your own mild government. (This example would rather fall under 4.) This I know that errors in a good government and in a bad are equally almost incident.—Col.:—Too ignorantly to deceav any reader but an unlerned.

B. Comparison.

1. In E. Mn. English the endings are the same as in late M. E., that is in the English of 1300—1500. But we have also the periphrastic comparison, by means of *more* and *most*, which appears already in Early M. E. At first, the two methods of comparison were used indiscriminately, and such comparisons as *more sad, most sad, beautifuller, beautifullest* were frequent in M. E., and even as late as the first half of the XVIIth century there existed no rule which might have been uniformly followed.[1]

Milton preferred the endings *er, est,* the use of which is more and more restricted in present English for reasons of euphonism. C. P. B. 53:—the two cheifest and ancientest universities.—Anim. 4:—the properest object; 6, the elegantest authors; 16, the ancientest fathers.—Areop.:—a vision far ancienter; the ancientest fathers; accuratest thoughts; backwardest; diligentest writers; exactest things; look whether those places be the honester=(the) more honest; likeliest, loyalest, unwillingest.—L. to H.: — hopefullest, likest, usefullest; the likeliest means.—Doct. and Disc. of Div., Int.:—choisest, learnedst (and best learned); I, the equallest sense (equal in the sense of just—most just); II, chiefest, loneliest; III, sobrest; IV, unmeetest.— Of Ref. in Engl.:—famousest, chiefest, wickedest.

2. Adjectives with superlative meaning can, as a rule, not be compared. "Es sind dies diejenigen, welche an und für sich das höchste Mass des Begriffes, oder negative Bestimmungen ausdrücken. Doch wird der Superlativ mancher Wörter dieser Art zur Verstärkung der im Positiv enthaltenen Bedeutung gebraucht."[2] So Milton, C. P. B. 53:—cheifest.—Doct. and Disc. of Div.: — chiefest, loneliest.— Areop.:—sublimest.—The double comparative *lesser* is of frequent occurrence. Acc. Comm. Gr.:—If it be the proper name of a lesser place (einer kleineren Stadt).—Hobbes: — the lesser cities of Greece; many lesser commonwealths.

---

[1] Gill, Logon. Angl., Cap. IX, merely mentions the two methods, he does not discuss their application.
Cf. also Sweet, Op. cit. 326, 327.
[2] Mätzner, Engl. Gramm. III, 299.

3. *Irregular Comparison. a. Old, older (elder), oldest (eldest).* Milton frequently uses the archaic forms *elder, eldest,* where present English would require *older, oldest.* This is the case throughout in Acced. Comm. Gr. One instance in Areop. is:—our ancestors elder or later.—Browne, U. B.:—Carnall interment was of the elder date.

b. Far, farther, farthest (O. E. *feor, fierr(e), fyrra, fyrrest,*—later forms:—*fer, ferre, ferrest, feorrest; fer, furre, firre, ferrest).* Milton uses with the greatest regularity the comparative form *farre.*—L. to H.:— a farre country (4 times farre). — *Farre* is indeed the correct form; *th* seems to have got into the orthography of the word out of false analogy with *further.* Doct. and Disc. of Div. has also *farre.* Areop. 6 times.

In some cases we meet the form *furder, further* (O. E. comparative:—furdra [major], together with the adverb:—furdor [ulterius], connected with the adverb *fore, forth).*—Areop.:—the discours furder made; passing no furder; to gain furder in wors condition; no furder discussing.—C. P. B. 185: —furder.

c. Little, less, least. Here, too, we meet both, the present English superlative form *least* and the M. E. form *lest* (O. E. *lutel, litel,* — *lasse, las, lesse; leeste,* and *later, lest*). Ex. Areop.:—How they shall be lest hurtfull, how lest enticing.—But:—at least, upon every least breath.

d. Late, later, latest; (latter, last). The two forms *later,* in sequence of time, and *latter,* in sequence of place, distinct nowadays, seem to have been occasionally used the one for the other. Milton writes, for instance, in C. P. B. 221: —"Henry the seventh in his latter days."— Bacon, Adv. of L., p. 1: —"The former . . . the later," where we should expect "the latter."

e. Most, superlative of much, many, stands, as a rule, before plurals in the meaning of:—the greatest number; in O. E. however, *micel* meant "great," *mare, more* meant "greater," and *mast, mest, most* meant "greatest," and stood also before nouns in the singular. This old meaning seems to have been before Milton's mind, when he wrote in R. of C. G., preface:—"The most part aime not beyond the good of civill society."

4. The two members of a comparison are connected by the conjunction *then.* Modern *than* is not to be found in any one of the prose works which we have read through, nor in the extracts from Bacon, Hobbes, Herbert, Browne and Taylor. And yet in M. English we have already *than, thanne, thonne,* corresponding to O. E. þonne, þon, þan, by the side of *then, thenne, thene.* The form *then,* in Milton, is very likely a phonetic spelling.

CHAPTER VII.

Numerals.

Milton's use of them is generally in agreement with the rules now observed. Concerning the

A. Cardinal Numbers,

however, we may take note of the following peculiarities:—

1. The number *two* is regularly spelt *tow,* in the autograph pieces contained in "Ramblings."—Ex. 37:—his tow sons; 41, tow sons. Everywhere else regularly two:—Prel. Episc. 11:—two grave nurses.—

2. *Seven* is found spelt sometimes *seaven* (O. E. *seofon*), sometimes *seven.* Ex. Prel. Episc. 5:—to the seaven Bishops; the 7 sleepers that slept three hundred seaventy and two years.

3. *Hundred* is also spelt *hunderd.* Ex. Prel. Episc. 5:—a hunderd yeares his predecessor.

4. In cumulative numeral groups (twenty-five) the units always come first; just as in O. E. *fīf and twentig manna.* According to present use this may be done for the numbers up to fifty, provided that the tenths be not preceded by a stronger number.[1] Milton says:—L. to H.:—from twelve to one and twenty; three or four and twenty.—Areop.:—two and fifty degrees; five or six and twenty sees.

5. Gill tells us, Logon., p. 65:—In numeris compositis, major praecedit minorem, ut:—*twenty one, thirty two, forty three;* aut contra, minor majorem, ut:—*one and twenty, six and fifty, nine and fifty,* sed

---

[1] Mätzner, Engl. Grammatik, I, 301.

ulterius hanc formam non prosequeris. This he applies to the ordinal numbers, too, and goes as far as:—"*The nine and fiftieth*, tum cessa, posthac enim major praeponitur minori."

6. Cardinals may be used substantively:—C. P. B. 179:—upon a fifteen granted (on the granting of a fifteen); 220, the fifteens.

7. *Dozen* in the sense of twelve, in Prel. Episc. 5:—an offspring of some dozen epistles.

B. Ordinals.

1. Hodges, in his "Primrose" (last few pages, where numbers are taught), duly distinguishes cardinal from ordinal numbers ("expressing the order of any thing"), and says:—"These latter ought to have *(th)* set ôver the head for their distinction, but in printed books it is very seldom observed; you must therefore distinguish them only by the sense of the place wherein they are set." This was indeed the case not only in printed books, but also in MSS.; we found, for instance, in C. P. B. 182, 221:—Henry 3; 185 and 221, Richard 2; 242, Henry 5; but also:—74, Edward the 1; 185, Richard the 2 (2), and Henry 3^d; 221, Henry the 7th; Henry the 8th.

2. The ordinal number *fift* had already begun to be discarded at that period. But Milton uses both forms, *fifth* and *fift;* O. E. *fifta;* M. E. *fifte.* The form *fift* is to be found in Ram. 39:—the fift or sixt day; in Doct. and Disc. of Div. Bk. I, Cap. VI; in R. of C. G. I, 5; in Areop.:—fift essence; but, Eikon. 2:—in the fifth yeare. In late Mn. English *th* was again introduced, owing to the influence of the other numerals; so also in *sixt*, which Milton had kept as well.— C. P. B. 220:—the sixt of every mans goods;—Judgment of Bucer:— dedicated to Edward the sixt;—Anim. 14:—Edward the sixt.

Gill gives, p. 65:—fift, sixt.

CHAPTER VIII.

Pronouns.

A. Personal Pronouns.

1. Remnants of older inflexion cannot be said to occur in the printed works of Milton; but in Ram. and in C. P. B. we have come across the one form *thire*, in the ending *e* of which we should be inclined to see a trace of the M. E. gen. plur. "þeire;" we generally find it connected with a genitive. Ex. Ram. 39:—thire mistresse sorrow; thire maisters return (6); 40, in thire maisters defence; but nomin.: — thir maister.

The form þa=they was relatively recent in English grammar. The late O. E. tendency to confuse "hēo," "she," and "hīe," "they," under the common form "hēo," led to a more extended use of the demonstrative plural "þa," "they." In the M. E. period, this usage was especially developed in North-Thames English. But as "þa" also had the strong demonstrative meaning "those ones," "those," and as Scandinavian influence was strong in North-Thames English, "þa" in the sense of "they," was made into "þei" by the influence of Scandinavian "þeir," "they," where the *r* is only the inflection of the nom. masc. plur. The influence of the Scandinavian dat. and gen. plur. "þeim," "to them," "þeira," "their," also changed the old "þǣm, þāra" into "þeim, þeire, þeir" in North-Thames English. In late M. E. "þei" found then its way into the standard dialect.[1]

2. In the original form of the language and in standard M. E. *ye* is the nominative, *you* the accusative case. This distinction, however, was not kept by Elizabethan authors.—In Early Mn. English the objective form *you* came to be used as a nominative, and in present English *you* has completely supplanted *ye* in the spoken language.

Alexander Gill,[2] Milton's master, tells us that *ye* and *you* are to be used as nominative and vocative, *you* alone as accusative case;

---

[1] Sweet. New Engl. Grammar, p. 336.
[2] Cf. Logon., "Personalia," p. 37—40.

but, as a matter of fact, the associations between form and grammatical function were very unsettled in Milton's time. We can give numerous examples of *ye,* as well as of *you,* used both as nominative and objective case:—

a. *Ye* as subject (nominative).—Areop.:—Ye must reform it perfectly, which I know ye abhorre to doe. Yet, though ye should condescend to this. I find ye esteem it. If ye be resolved. To think ye were not. Ye professe. Ye have the inventors ript up. Ye like not. Ye were importuned. All men who know how ye honour truth will clear yee (accusative) readily. Though ye take from a covetous man all his treasure, he has yet one jewell left, ye cannot bereave him of his covetousnesse. Ye cannot make. them chaste. Ye remove them both alike. Ye must repeale all scandalous books. After ye have drawn them up. What nation it is whereof ye are. What should ye doe?—But:—You must then first become that which ye cannot be. L. to H.:—Ye shall have.—Col.:—Yee see what a desiner wee have him.—But:—If you bring limitations.—The form *ye* by far prevails.

b. *Ye* as objective case. Them that praise yee are known by ye. Many who honour ye. He gives ye. To thinke ye pleased. They shall observe yee. Renders ye willing. Shall lay before ye.

B. Possessive Pronouns.

1. In M. E. a distinction was made between the conjoint "min, þin," and "mi, þi;" "min, þin" dropping their final *n* before a consonant. This distinction was still kept up, to some extent, in Early Mn. E., but the shorter forms came more and more into use. Milton makes a most scanty use of mine, thine. The only instances of *mine* found, are in Anim. 16:—I shall justifie mine own assertion;—Prel. Episc.:—what mine author says;—Doct. and Disc. of Div., Cap. VI:—Mine author sung it to me;—Areop.—Mine owne acquittall.

2. The possessive form *its* was scarcely yet admitted into literary English. Cf. Morris, E. Acc., § 172. This form is not much older than the end of the XVIth century. It is not found in the Bible, nor in Spenser; rarely in Shakespeare and Bacon, more frequently in Milton, who, however, preferred *his.* Ex. Areop.:—That other clause which we thought had died with his brother.

C. Demonstrative Pronouns.

Here follows an instance of the demonstrative force of the personal pronoun *them,* which Mätzner, I, 322, rightly qualifies as a dialectical peculiarity. Areop.:—Them that praise ye are known to ye.—In Early English:—*hi, hii* (plural of personal pronoun *he*), *hem,* as well as "þa, þo," belonged distinctly to the class of demonstratives. Cf. Rob. of Gloucester:—Hii of Denemarch flowe sone (p. 378). Fram hem of Denemarche (I, 295).

D. Relative Pronouns.

1. Regarding the general use of the relatives *who, which, that,* in Milton's time, no definite rule can be given. *Who* is but rarely met in the writers of the first half of the XVIIth century (except, of course, as an interrogative pronoun); *that* and *which* indifferently refer to singular and plural antecedents of all genders; *what* is used in the sense of *that which,* as it is in our days. In a great number of cases the relative pronouns are omitted.—Milton, R. of C. G., Bk. II, pref.:—He who hath obtained, &c., and in the same sentence:—He that hath obtained; to them that will.—Hobbes, Lib. of Sub., Cam. Ser., seems to prefer *that.* Ex. that=who:—the giver that was not bound; one that was free; to him that could see; he that so dieth; I have seen a man that had another man, &c.; which=whom:—a strong monarch which they abhorre.—Browne, Rel. Med., Cam. Ser.:— the scepticks that affirmed; the duke of Venice that weds.—But Milton, Bucer:—to them who know what wise men, &c.

Who as a relative is not recognised by Ben Johnson, who speaks of "one relative:—which," that, during the XIIth century, began to supply the place of the indeclinable relative *the,* and, in the XIVth century, it was the ordinary though not the only relative. In the XVIth century, *which* often supplied its place, and in the XVIIth century *who* was *occasionally* employed instead of *it.*—At a later period, Addison's time, *that* had again come into fashion and had almost driven *who* and *which* out of use.[1]

---

[1] Morris. Outl. of English Accid., p. 130.

Gill says that *who, whom* and *which* may always be rendered by
that:—"Sic verti potest:—He who cannot contain himself:—

Sing. 1. He which cannot contain himself.

2. He that cannot contain himself.

Plur. 1. They who cannot contain themselves.

2. They which cannot contain themselves.

3. They that cannot contain themselves.

Objective case:—

1. I accuse him whom I know to be guilty.

2. I accuse him which I know to be guilty.

3. I accuse him that I know to be guilty."[1]

2. The use of a *relative pronoun ruled by a preposition* is an exception in Milton's writings. We notice also that, as a rule, pronominal relative clauses are introduced by "a compound of the adverbs of place "where," or "there," and the preposition. Ex. C. P. B. 220:—
The which the king knowing the cause whereof instantly pardon'd.

Areop.:—The subject whereon I entered. The liberty whereof this discourse will be a testimony. A fit instance wherein to show such as shall be thereto appointed. A life whereof there is no great losse. A massacre whereof the execution ends not in . . . He fell to the study of that whereof he was so scrupulous. In witnesse whereof I have given. Whereof what better witness can ye expect. To ordain wisely as in this world of evill, in the midd'st whereof God hath plac't us. I should produce useful drugs wherewith to temper med'cins. Wherefore did he create passions within us. A councel wherein bishops were forbid. This is the prime service wherein this order should give proof of itself. This is what I had to show wherein this order cannot conduce to that end whereof it bears the intention. The mortall glasse wherein we contemplate. The commonwealth wherein he was born. In a hand scars legible whereof three pages would not down. Consider what nation it is whereof ye are and whereof ye are the governours. A vertue whereof none can participate but greatest and wisest men. The order would be fruitlesse to that order whereto ye meant it. Another reason whereby to make it plain. Christ urg'd it as where-.

---

[1] Gill. Logon., "Personalia," p. 37—40.

with to justifie himself. That piece of ground whereon Hannibal him - self encampt.

L. to H.:—For the want whereof this nation perishes. The w ay whereby we may best hope to give account. The studies wherewit h they close the dayes work. The gropes of wrastling wherein Engli sh men were wont to excell. This will be enough wherein to prove th eir strength. The praxis thereof.

Acc. Comm. Gr.:—Adjectives may form comparison wher eof there be two degrees. Borrow from the verb wherof they are derived. Words following the substantive wherof they are spoken. Governing . . . wherby one part of speech is governed by another.

Prel. Episc.:—An allegation wherin we see . . . In some treatises one whereof goes under the name . . . The difference wherin I wonder . . .

Anim. 5: — Wherefore should you begin with the Devils name? 8. Wherby they might be the abler to discover . . . 15. Wherfore have you sate still?

What strikes us as *archaic and peculiar,* in many of the above examples, is the fact that the relative clauses are related to substan- tives; their being related to whole sentences is of frequent occurrence. Mätzner says with respect to these sentences[1]: — "Die Beziehung rela- tiver Ortsadverbien auf Substantivbegriffe ist eine über viele Sprachen verbreitete Erscheinung und reicht bis ins Angelsächsische. Be vor die interrogativen Formen als relative verwendet wurden, galten die Demonstrativen dafür. Bei vielen alten Schriftstellern gehen beide Formen (where, there) neben einander her." From the above examples it will be seen that the interrogative form *where* had superseded the demonstrative *there,* which occurs but rarely. Forms like "this which I speake of" (Bacon:—Of true Greatnesse, &c., Cam. Ser.) are not found in Milton, he would no doubt have said:—*whereof.*—But Bacon says also (Adv. of L.):—This spice the mixture whereof will make knowledge soveraign; the end whereof will consist of the summer; that light whereby he may reveal unto himselfe the nature of God.

Browne has (Rel. Med., Cam. Ser.):—The rhetoricke where- with I persuade another; when he had not subdued the halfe of any part thereof.

---

[1] Mätzner. Engl. Gramm. III, 547.

3. Milton often uses the relative *which* with repeated antecedent; this construction is now considered as archaic and is only adopted where great definiteness is desired,—in official, legal documents which have retained in every language a quaint style of their own,—or where care must be taken to select the right antecedent.—Doct. and Disc. of Div., Cap. V:—From which words (a quotation from the Bible) so plain lesse cannot be concluded.—Of Ref. in England, Lib. II:—In which attempt if they fall short (of bringing the law under the wardship of Lust and Will); wins the exarchat of Ravenna, which though it had been a possession; their treason to the Royall blood, which had it tooke effect.—Prel. Episc.:— It being the only book left us of Divine authority, through all which booke can be no where found, &c.; entitling him Archbishop of Antioch Theopolis, which name of Theopolis.—R. of C. G., Bk. I, Int.:—Which thing (reasons of church government) further to explane, I shall no longer deferre.— "Sometimes a noun of similar meaning supplants the antecedent" (Abbott, § 269), sometimes, too, as seen above (Ref. in England, &c.), a pronoun takes its place.

This use of which is due to Latin influence, where the relatives "qui, quae, quod" are constantly used thus, in a demonstrative sense, that is:—pointing, referring again to that which has been mentioned, in order to bring it more vividly before the mind of the reader.[1] *Which* has here a distinctly demonstrative force and stands for *and that, that indeed.*

E. Reflexive Pronouns.

1. *a.* In Early English the emphatic adjective *self* (Anglo-Saxon *sylf*=same), is added to nouns and personal pronouns, being generally inflected like a strong adjective in agreement with its headword. *" God self hit ʒeworhte."*—*Self* does not make a pronoun reflexive, but simply emphasizes one that is already so. By degrees however, the combination of *self* with a personal pronoun was restricted to the reflexive meaning, the simple pronouns being restricted to the non-reflexive meaning; and, in the XIIIth century, when the genitive

---

[1] Cf. Cicero, Cato major, 6:—Quam palmam utinam dii immortales tibi reservent.—Cicero, de Imp. Pomp., 15:—Qui quo die . . ., &c.—Contra quem qui exercitus duxerunt, ii senatus singulares honores decrevit.

was substituted for the dative of the prefixed pronoun in the first and second person, — "mi self, þi self" for "me self, þe self," "our self, your self" for "us self, you self,"—*self* came to be regarded as a substantive,[1] and made its plural like nouns ending in *f, fe*.

Milton, no doubt, considered it as such, for he separated it as a rule from the personal pronoun. Ex. Areop.:—I might defend my selfe. Partiall to your selves. He durst venture himselfe. A debate with himselfe. We must not expose our selves. Truth opens her self faster. The service wherin this order should give proof of it selfe. Love lerning for it self. When I have disclosed my self. We are so timorous of our selves. And from thence derives it self. In some disconformity to our selves. Without being unlike her self. Lest we should devote our selves to set places. — Col:—I composed my self to read.— L. to H.:—Though a linguist should pride himselfe. To advance it selfe. Every man can count him selfe.

b. In the following examples Milton uses *self,* not with a reflexive meaning, but simply as a means to emphasis. Areop.:—Not so inferior as your selves are superior. He kills reason it selfe. The breath of reason it selfe. The Bible it selfe must remove out of the world. We our selves esteem not of that obedience. If we our selves condemn not our teaching. We look not into the sun it selfe. The reforming of Reformation it self. The book it self will tell us more. — Acc. Comm. Gr.:—The positive signifieth the thing it self.—Col.:— If your self be not guilty.—L. to H.:—To be won from pleasure it selfe. — *Himself* alone is regularly spelt in one word, whereas *my self, our selves, your selves, it self,* mostly occur written in two words, which proves that Milton was quite conscious of the meaning of *self;* *themselves* is written both ways. There is nothing reflective in *self,* the reflective force belongs altogether to the pronoun to which it is appended, or, properly speaking, lies in the verb which expresses the reflected action.

c. In E. and M. English the personal pronouns alone were used reflexively, and had not ceased to be used as such as late as Milton's time. He offers a few instances of this reflexive force of personal pronouns:—Doct. and Disc. of Div., Int.:—Let him bethink him

---

[1] Sweet. New Engl. Grammar, p. 346.

withall.—Areop.:—They will mak' em and cut' em out what religion ye please ('*em* *hem* now superseded by *them*).—L. to H.:—Some betake them to state affairs.—R. of C. G., I, Cap. 5:—He repents him.

2. Milton's contemporaries, too, considered *self* rather as a substantive. Hobbes always separates:—*it selfe* (but *himself*); Herbert, Walton, Taylor likewise. Browne writes *himselfe*, but *our selves, my self, it self;*—Rel. Med.:—their third or fourth selves;—U. B.:—the fame of their passed selves.

F. Indefinite Pronouns.

1. *Either*. There seems to be considerable uncertainty in the use and meaning of *either*. It is of O. E. origin:—aégðer -each of two, Lat. *uterque,* both, the meaning *one of two,* Lat. *alteruter,* being expressed by:—"æghwæþer," shortened to "áuþer, áþer." In M. E. the pronoun "áuþer" was gradually disused, and "eiþer" was used to express both meanings.—In Mn. E. *either* is now mostly restricted to the alternative meaning *alteruter.* Milton does not make that restriction yet, he uses *either* in both senses.—In Par. Lost. I, 243, he says, for instance:— "Spirits, when they please, can either sex assume or both," where *either* must mean not:—the one *and* the other, but the one *or* the other, otherwise *both* has no meaning. So also in Col.:—"'Tis true, that to divorce upon extreme necessity, when through the perversnes, or the apparent unfitnes of either, the continuance can bee to both no good at all."

But in other passages Milton clearly uses the word in the sense of *each,* i. e. both of them, as Par. Lost. V, 130:—"She silently a gentle tear let fall from either eye, and wiped them with her hair."— A tear from each eye justifies the plural *them.* So in Col.:—"Many persons, gracious both, may yet happ'n to bee very unfitly married to the great disturbance of either," i. e. *each.* Again, Areop.:—"He who eats or eats not, regards a day or regards it not, may do either to the Lord." This however is slightly puzzling:—the meaning which we may derive from the text in the Bible is that "he may do *both*" to the Lord. This sentence would have been clearer if the subject had been expressed distinctively, and separately, perhaps thus:— "He who eats or eats not, he who regards a day or regards it not may do either (i. e. one of the two, any one) to the Lord."

2. *Several* has the same form in M. E. and in Old French; it comes from the Latin *separa(bi)lis*, corresponding to the Old Latin *separabilis* = separable, separate. It is now used in the plural, for the English word *sundry*, O. E. *synderig singularis, sundrie, sondry;* it occurs, however, sometimes as a singular in older writers in the sense of *separate* (Alc. hefde sindri moder, Lay. I, 114); so in Milton:—"The just retaining of each man his severall copy" (Areop.); again in the sense of *separate*, but in the plural, Doct. and Disc. of Div.:—"Must look for two several oppositions."

3. *Each other.* The reciprocal noun-pronouns *each other*, one another, are now inseparable compounds, but their elements were originally separate words with independent inflections; this was un-doubtedly the more correct construction, for, in the sentence "Love each other," the meaning and true construction is:—"Each love the other," so that *each* is subject and *other* the object. Thus also was it construed in O. E. when *other* always took the inflectional ending required by the syntax. Ex.:—"Hí cwædon ælc to óðorum" (Ev. Marci, IV, 41). In E. M. English this inflection was frequently dropped:—"Heo wold ever ælc oðer halden for broðr" (Lay. Brut. 5163). In Milton we find a reminiscence of the original construction in:—"They are seen complementing and ducking each to other" (Areop.).—Doct. and Disc. of Div.:—created so different each from other.—Cf. Taylor, β:—to warre one against another.

4. *Enough*, O. E. *genóh, ynough, enow, anow,* is always spelt *anough* and *anow* in Milton. O. Fries. *anoegh*, and Got. *ganoh*, likewise contain *a*.

CHAPTER IX.

The Article.

A.

1. There is no observation to be made on the use of the two articles by Milton:—*the* being the definite article, *a, an* the indefinite article before words beginning with a consonant, and a vowel respec-tively. Ex. Anim.:—a rougher accent; a grand imposture; a grim

laughter; an austere visage; an outlandish name; an episcopacy;—
Prel. Episc.:—a boy; a bishop; a church; a man; a member; an
allegation; an unknown table; an exact account. We may give but
few instances of the use of *an* before a word beginning with *u*, i. e.
with a half consonant, when present English would prefer *a*. C. P.
B. 183:—An word to Henry 3; 160, a spirit to free an nation;—
L. to H.:—An universal insight into things.—But in Doct. and Disc.
of Div. we find in accordance with the now prevailing use:—such a
one;—Anim. 2:—such a one; — Areop.:—a heretick.

2. Milton's contemporaries did not consider *h aspirate* as a consonant, and consequently used the form *an,* of the indefinite article,
indifferently before words beginning with an *h aspirate* and *h mute*.
Hobbes, Lib. of Subj., Cam. Ser.:—a man with an head.—Browne,
U. B.:—an hair of his head; an hundred pounds of oyntment; an
handsome anticipation of heaven; which, being not only an hope.—
Bacon, Of the true Greatness, &c., Cam. Ser.:—an handfull of people;—
Hy. VII, Cam. Ser.:—Hee was of an high mind; hee led an happy
warfare.—An explanation for this lies perhaps in the remark which
Mr. R. Grant White, in his "Memorandums on English pronunciation
in the Elizabethan Era" (an appendix to the 12th vol. of his Shakespeare, ed. 1861), writes on the letter *H*; he simply says:—"*H* probably more often dropped (in pronunciation) than at present."

B.

As to the syntactical use of the article, however, we may take
note of many a peculiarity.

1. The Definite Article.

a. Cases in which the article is placed contrary to present use:—

α. Milton occasionally places the definite article before the
superlative *most*. Doct. and Disc. of Div.:—The most disciples after
him; the most of men;—Areop.:—superior to the most of them.
But:—We are to send our thanks to heaven louder then most of
nations.

β. As a rule the definite article is now omitted before the names
of titles, when they are followed by a proper name. But we find in

Milton:—"the Lord Brooke" (Areop.). This unique case is easily explained:—Milton only wishes to bring out this name of "Lord Brook" with emphasis:—"Ye know him I am sure; yet I for honours sake shall name him, the Lord Brook;" it may be interpreted thus:—"That well-known Lord Brook, Lord Brook you know so well." (Cf. use of the article in the French sentence:—"Faust, tragédie de Gœthe," and "Faust, la tragédie de Gœthe.")

γ. *The* used before a comparative becomes an adverb, as in *the more, the less;* it is the old instrumental *thi* of the demonstrative pronoun *se,* and corresponds to the Latin "eo" in "eo magis." This *the* is now dropped when a second adverb precedes the comparative, (much better, much more). We should therefore prefer to say *much rather* (multo magis), instead of the archaic *much the rather* which Milton still uses (Doct. and Disc. of Div., Introd.).

δ. Instead of *on the sudden* (L. to H.), we should now rather say *on a sudden, of a sudden,* with the indefinite article.— Bacon, too, uses the definite article in: —"Upon the suddaine."

b. Cases in which the definite article is omitted contrary to present use.

α. The function of the definite article being to determine a noun by means of its individualising power, the nature and the syntactical relations of the substantive alone can be taken into consideration, when we are to decide as to the omission of the article, or as to its use.—We may here distinguish two cases:—

1. The article is to be used whenever a noun denotes a distinctly determined object, or an object which may be considered as being distinctly determined; thus, in the course of speech it is to be used with words which, by themselves, would not require it, as soon as these words are made to denote distinctly determined objects by means of individualising additions, attributes, relative sentences, and even in consequence of their mere relation to the rest of the sentence.—We should say, in present English:—"will is a mental activity," but:—"the Divine will can be traced in nature," "the will of this man." Milton, however, speaks in Doct. and Disc. of Div., Introd., of *Divine will;* he likewise omits the article before words like *God, sin, man,* though they be accompanied by adjectives, or distinctly

determined. Again, Doct. and Disc. of Div., Cap. II:—Not beseeming
either Christian profession, or morall conversation; III, dishonourable
to Christian doctrine;—Areop.:—It had been partiall to correct him
for grave Cicero and not for scurrill Plautus; they cannot be hindered
by all the licencing that sainted inquisition could ever yet contrive;
a wise man will make better use of an idle pamphlet then a fool
will doe of sacred scripture.

The omission of the article in expressions like:—"Divine providence," "ancient Rome" (Areop.) can, however, be justified, if we
consider that we are adding to the noun words which denote qualities
and attributes inherent to its notion, forming, as it were, part of the
substantive.

2. *Second case.* The article is omitted whenever a noun does not
denote a definite object, where we do not individualise; this is the
case when we are using collective names, abstract names, names of
species standing in the plural.—Milton generally writes in accordance
with these rules, yet he goes beyond the present use when, in C. P.
B., for instance, he repeatedly omits the article:—

a. before surnames given to kings:—180, 220, in Edward Confessors time; 181, William Conqueror, (but 179, Edward the Confessor);

b. in 182, 221, Henry 3; 185, 221, Richard 2, (on the same
page, however, we find Richard the second); 220, 221, Henry 3^d;
242, armie of Henry 5; but 221, Henry the 7th; Henry the 8th; 243,
Richard the first.

Milton makes an exceptional use of the definite article in this
sentence:—"A man may be a heretick in the truth" (Areop.). *The*
is used here in order to avoid a misunderstanding; the sense is:—
a heretick as regards truth, with respect to truth, and not:—in truth
indeed.

β. Milton frequently omits the definite article after *all,* not only
in the plural, but even in the singular. C. P. B. 182:—all churches
are the popes;—Doct. and Disc. of Div., Introd.:—Chase away all
truth and solid wisdome out of humane life;—Areop.:—We must
regulate all recreations and pastimes; while bishops were to be baited

down, then all presses might be open. — Mätzner says[1]: — "Notwendig
ist der Artikel nach *all* seit ältester Zeit nicht; er hängt von den auch
sonst erforderlichen Bedingungen für den Artikel ab. Analog ist das
Verfahren der romanischen Sprachen beim fr. *tout* (toute vérité), it.
tutto, wie beim gr. πᾶς, goth. *alls*: — "alla so hairda" (Matth. 8, 31).
Die quantitative Bestimmung wird als die wesentliche angesehen,
während der Artikel dem Substantivbegriffe nur noch eine Bezeich-
nung nach aussen gibt, welche unter Umständen wegfallen muss oder
kann." — Now, in the second and third of the above examples *all* is
indeed used in the sense of French *tout*=each, every one. In the
first example, we have the usual omission of the article before an
abstract word; present English however would require the article: —
"all the truth."

γ. The definite article is frequently dropped before superlatives.
In E. Mn. E. this is mostly the case when a genitive in the plural
follows the superlative; Milton, however, makes it a general rule in
his prose writings. — Doct. and Disc. of Div., Introd.: — The purity
of God to be cleer'd from foulest imputations. What wonder if we
fall into the subjection of worst and deadliest offences. V, men here-
tofore of greatest name in vertue. — L. to H.: — Men of most approved
wisdom, and some of highest authority (*the* would be required before
most, because it does not stand alone before *wisdom*, it is accompanied by *approved*, and simply forms the superlative of *approved*).
The acts of ripest judgment. At first comming. Tragedies of statliest
and most regal argument. The society of those who are best and
most eminent. According to best wishes. — Areop.: — When greatest
likelihoods are brought. It is of greatest concernment. Yet best and
wisest commonwealths through all ages, and falsest seducers were
the first who tooke it up. Julian the Apostat and suttlest enemy to
our faith. To do sharpest justice on books. The Bible brings in holiest
men murmuring against Providence. Those books which are likeliest,
&c. . . . Books of grossest infamy. These they be which will bear
chief sway. In what book of greatest consequence. The orphan re-
mainders of worthiest men. He shall assume these now over worthiest
and excellentest books and ablest authors that write them. Who can

---

1 Mätzner. Engl. Grammatik III, 180.

discern those stars of brightest magnitude. Taken up with the study of highest and most important matters. The search of greatest and exactest things. To redresse willingly what hath bin erred, and to esteem a plain advertisement more then others have done a sumptuous bribe, is a vertue whereof none can participat but greatest and wisest men.—Col.:—To my freinds of which may fewest bee so unhappy.

"Der artikellose Superlativ mit dem Genitiv," says Mätzner,[1] "ist in alter Zeit sehr geläufig; er findet sich aber selten, wo er in Zahl und Fall mit dem Hauptwort kongruiert, ohne Artikel;" the more striking, then, is this omission of the article in Milton. Mätzner then goes on to say:—"Der Superlativ legt einem Individuum, oder einer Anzahl von Individuen unter einer Gesamtgattung, eine Eigenschaft im höchsten Grade bei. Der Superlativ ist seit frühester Zeit nicht schlechthin an den bestimmten Artikel gebunden, welchen er überhaupt da nicht zu sich nimmt, wo eine andere determinative Bestimmung diesen ausschliesst; doch hat er, wo das letztere nicht der Fall ist, im attributiven Verhältnisse die Neigung zur Verbindung mit demselben, da durch den Artikel die Ausscheidung eines bestimmten Individuums, oder einer Klasse, aus der Gattung entschieden zur Anschauung gebracht wird."—But, looking at it closely, we may find that there is nothing very definite about a superlative; how far, we may ask, is a quality attributed to a person or thing in the highest degree? This "highest degree" is a notion which depends on a great number of more or less known and definite factors; they lie at some distance from us, their exact value is not always appreciable. Take the last sentence from Areop.:—"greatest and wisest men." Who are they? How many are there? Where do their greatness and their wisdom begin and end?—There is something vague, general about it; certainly Milton does not know them all. Quite a different meaning is given by the addition of the article:—"the greatest and the wisest men;" we should feel that Milton has in his mind a certain definite class or number of men, worthy to be called "wisest and greatest." Every one of the above examples might be analysed in a similar way, and that would prove that Milton had his reason for

---

[1] Engl. Grammatik III, 298.

omitting so regularly the definite article before superlatives. — Bacon, too, says, for instance (Adv. of L.): — With most blessed and happie fruit of marriage. — So Herbert (Hist. of Geo.): — Without least shew of pitie.

2. The Indefinite Article.

a. Milton frequently omits the indefinite article before abstract words, even when they are accompanied by an attribute; it may be for shortness' sake. Doct. and Disc. of Div.: — Needs not long enquiry; contriving matter of continual sorrow; — L. to H.: — Such as have the worth to make triall; — Areop.: — When great reformation is expected; — Ready and Easy way: — I trust I shall have spoken persuasion to abundance of sensible men.

b. That is also the case before the adjective or indefinite pronoun *other.* — Areop.: — Neither he nor other inspired author; without knowing other reason; — Doct. and Disc. of Div., Introd.: — Whoso preferrs either matrimony, or other ordinance; — Eikon. 2: — For other manner of prescribing was not suspected.

c. The indefinite article is omitted after *so,* in Doct. and Disc. of Div. I: — Though never to so good intention. — Hobbes, too, omits it after *such:* — Although few perceive that such government is not government (Lib. of Sub.).

d. Some uncertainty may be noticed in the use and in the omission of the indefinite article after *what.* In present English *what* is followed by the indefinite article in exclamations, whereas the article is omitted in questions. Such a sentence as the following one is not quite clear to us (Areop.): — "And to what an author this violence hath bin lately done, and in what book of greatest consequence, I could now instance." We should expect either: — "and to what author, and in what book," where *what* would simply be a relative, or then: — "and to what an author, and in what a book."

CHAPTER X.

Particles.

A. Adverbs.

I. Substantive Adverbs.

1. Adverbs with case endings. The two forms *needs* (gen. sing.) and *alwayes* (old acc.) have alone been found. The dative form *ever* generally stands in the place of modern "always." O. E. *æfre.* Ex. Anim. 7:—This hath bin ever so; 8, that ever attends them.—*Ever* occurs throughout in C. P. B. The accusative *meanwhile* is replaced in Ram. 36, by:—*in the mean.*—Herbert has (Hist. of Geo.):—all wayes.

2. Prepositional substantive adverbs. Ex. Ram. 39:—in the mean while; 40, at length;—Anim. 1:—before hand; by this meanes; 5, at this present; 3, oft times; 10, some times (2);—Eikon. 6:—in the mean while;—Prel. Episc.:—at this time.—Taylor, α:—in room of; β, in the mean time.—Hobbes (Hu. Nat.):—divers times.

II. Adjectival Adverbs.

1. Adverbs of manner are, as a rule, formed by the addition of *ly* to the adjective, so Ram. 40:—singularly;—C. P. B. 220:—worthyly; 221, unholilie; 243, unholilie set out, with monie dishonourably and impiously got;—Anim. 6:—gladly; 11, verily; 14, onely;—Prel. Episc. 1:—injuriously; 3, lastly, anciently, modernly, lightly;—Eikon.:— smoothly;—R. of C. G.:—intirely.—*Gladly* has a comparative:— *gladlier*, Areop.:—There is not any burden that some would gladlier post off to another.

2. Adjectives were then more freely used as adverbs, without any ending. It is true that some of those adverbs which have the same form as adjectives are the descendants of the Early English adverbs in *e,* and when this final *e* was dropped, the distinction between the adjective *hard*, for instance, and the adverb *hard(e)* was lost.

7

Others however are adverbs of manner to which, according to present use, the ending *ly* ought to have been added. This omission of an ending in the XVIIth century may be due:—1. to the fact that these adverbs are new formations on the analogy of the former adverbs; 2. to the influence of Old French, in which the uninflected forms of adjectives—originally the neuter singular—were used as adverbs. Ex. Areop.:—We find repeatedly the adverb *sure* (surely); sure they have a conceit; God sure esteems the growth of one vertuous person;— Col.:—Alter, it cannot sure.

Areop., *scars*=scarcely:—in a hand scars legible.

Certain certainly:—but certain, if execution be remisse.

Light=lightly:—I cannot set so light by.

Other instances, Acced. Comm. Gr.:—Verbs betokening want pass *direct* into an ablative; —L. to H.: —*Exceeding close*;—Doct. and Disc. of Div., Introd.:—No effect of tyranny can sit more *heavy* on the commonwealth; let this therfore be *new* examined (examined anew); Cap. VI, *wondrous* like him; he determines *plain* enough.

3. Adverbs, too, may take a "qualifying" *e*. In Milton, Bacon, Browne, and others, we find:—againe, indeede, onely; the latter word is spelt throughout with an *e*, which was no doubt kept as a sign of the length of the preceding *o*.

4. The adjective forms:—*first, last, next, most* are also used as adverbs:—Ram. 39:—at length a servant relates the truth and *last* he himselfe comes;—Eikon. 1:—those *most* in favour with him; those *most* his favorites.

5. Bacon, too, uses *sure*. Of true Greatn., Cam. Ser.:—the rather, *sure*.—*Scarce:*—He was *scarce* indulgent.—Herbert, Hist. of Geo.:— He judged himself *right* blessed; *exceeding* exact.—Taylor, α:—It is not *safe* ventured to present him; β, I had as good plow the sand; he had scarce learned.—Browne, U. B.:— to lie *soft*.

6. On the other hand, we came repeatedly across forms which were then still used as adjectives and adverbs as well, but which we should now consider as adverbs only; another proof of the unsettled state of the language. Acced. Comm. Gr.:—By reason of the *much* variety in declension;—Doct. and Disc. of Div., Cap. VI:—a lesse breach of wedlock.—Bacon, Adv. of L.:—th' aspiring to overmuch knowledge.—The word *ill*, which is now either an adverb, or, in a restricted meaning, an adjective to be used but predicatively, is found both attributively and predicatively used. Ex. Doct. and Disc. of Div. VI:—an ill mariage;—Prel. Episc.:—an ill hue; an ill look; an ill layd comparison.—Hobbes, Lib. of Sub., Cam. Ser.:—the ill quality.—Herbert, Hist. of Geo.:—their ill opinions.

III. Adverbs formed from Particles.

1. *Prepositional. After* is used in the sense of "afterwards" in C. P. B. 114:—after with great fury rejected (O. E. *æft-er*); 220, it was after by others permitted.

2. *Pronominal adverbs.* They are connected with the stems *he, the, who.* Ram. 39:—they hasten thither;—Prel. Episc. 8:—never the lesse.—*The* = O. E. "þî" is the instrumental case of *the* used as an adverb before comparatives.

C. P. B. 182:—from thence; *from* might have been dropped, *thence* alone indicating the origin by means of the genitive ending *ce* (es), which came in about the XIIIth century.—Prel. Episc. 9:—from whence.—Eikon. 3:—from thenceforth.

B. Prepositions.

1. Milton's use of prepositions is very unsettled. We frequently come across constructions which strike us as being very anomalous; frequently, too, we find that the preposition is omitted, and this is due either to the influence of the Latin construction required by a verb, or substantive, or adjective, or then it is omitted for shortness' sake, and owing to Milton's feeling that the preposition is implied in the notion of the word on which the attribute depends.

α. Examples:—*of.* Areop.:—For such Plato was provided of (pres. construct.:—provided with, Lat.:—providus alicujus rei, gen.). Ye cannot make us lesse pursuing of the truth. — *Behind* is constructed with *of* in:—There is yet behind of what I purposed to lay open.— *Of* is placed after *most,* contrary to present use, in:—louder then most of nations.—Again in:—we esteem not of that obedience which is of force, we may recognize the Latin construction "censere de aliqua re."

Of is omitted in such sentences as:—whatever sort the books be; what is to be thought of reading books, what ever sort they be; what sort books were prohibited; *what sort, what ever sort,* being equal to the Latin *quicunque.*—The Latin syntax may account for the omission of *of* in the following cases:—Areop.:—Protagoras himselfe was banisht the territory, *expellere* being frequently constructed with the ablative, without preposition;—I would not despair the greatest design,—cf. Latin:—*desperat et diffidit rebus suis* (Cic.), *suis fortunis desperat* (Cæs.), *nihil desperandum est* (Horace).—"Worthy so excellent a man," reminds us forcibly of the Latin:—*dignus aliqua re.* So Doct. and Disc. of Div.:—To expedite these knots were worthy a learned and memorable synod.

Of is omitted after *both* in Doct. and Disc. of Div. I:—both which.—Note also the use of *from out* instead of *out of,* in:—It was from out the rinde of one apple tasted . . . (Areop.).

We find in Milton's Bible:—"Six a clock" (1646), a phonetic spelling; also "before 3 of the clock" (1652).[1]

β. *By* is omitted in Areop.:—"Ye were importuned the passing of it." Cf. obstrepere alicui aliqua re; Cic.:—litteris mihi obstrepit.

γ. Milton is likewise influenced by the Latin construction when he writes:—"To prefer a thing before another," Lat. *prae*-ferre;— Doct. and Disc. of Div. VII:—God preferres the free worship of a Christian before the grievous observance of an unhappy marriage;— Areop.:—A dram of well-doing should be preferred before many times as much the forcible hindrance of evill-doing;—and also when he construes:—Areop.:—The adversarie waits the hour *(expectare aliquam rem);* as it was a thing slight and obvious to think on *(cogitare de aliqua re).*

δ. Sometimes, for shortness' sake, one preposition is wrongly used with two substantives, which cannot, separately, be construed with the same. Areop.:—"This licencing had reference and dependence to many other proviso's;" we must construe:—*reference to and*

---

[1] Cf. Jörss, p. 17, VI. Mätzner (II, 1, 279).

dependence on. "Encompassed and surrounded with his protection;" we should say:—*encompassed by and surrounded with,* or *by* also.

The preposition *of* is put but once in:—"Of other sects and the denying of providence they tooke no heed" (Areop.); and in:—"One of desert sufficient and ability either to do all, or to oversee it done" (L. to H.). We should now repeat the preposition before "the denying" and "ability."—Eikon. 9:—Averse to all his Parliament and both the nations of this iland.

2. The following examples of an anomalous use of prepositions were found in a few pages of Hobbes, Lib. of Subj., Cam. Ser.:—"in order to the good" instead of "for the good."— Cf. Milton, Areop.:—"on purpose to a life beyond life," instead of "for a life." "There is no soveraignty by the Ghostly," *by* in the sense of ("except") *besides.* We should now say:—"a house by the river, besides, by the side of the river;" "he was standing by me," "by my side," but we should not use *by* in this sense with abstract words.

C. Conjunctions.

1. The conjunction *that* is frequently omitted in such sentences as:—Areop.:—Seeing every nation affords not experience;—Prel. Episc.:—Seeing therefore some men have had so little care; R. of C. G.:—Which is so hard that we may see it is not for every learned man. — So Hobbes:—Seeing there is no commonwealth ; seeing it is manifest. —Browne:—We all hold there is a number of Elect and may be saved.—We notice that the principal clause always contains a verb expressing:—to see, to believe, to think, — and the corresponding verbs in Latin were generally construed with the accusative and infinitive. So Hobbes, Hu. Nat.:—Seeing the organs are in equal temper.

2. *When as.* We must make a distinction here:—

a. As was sometimes affixed to certain relative words to give greater precision of meaning; *whenas*= *just when.* Compare Greek δή in ἐπειδή. Milton gives us frequent instances of this pleonastic use of *as*:—Areop.:—"When as private persons are animated to thinke ye better pleased." Cf., too, Jörss, p. 18, VII, 1. Doct. and Disc. of

Div. II:—"It is a greater blessing from God whenas the solace of the mind is regarded before the sensitive pleasing of the body."

b. Whenas may also stand for present English *whereas,* and be used in adversative clauses. Areop.:—"It stops but one breach of licence, whenas those corruptions which it seeks to prevent, break in faster."—Doct. and Disc. of Div. III:—"How vaine is it that the vessell of voluptuous enjoyment must be made good, &c. . . . whenas the mind shall be thought good enough . . ." "They who have lived most loosely prove most successfull in their matches . . . whenas the sober man may easily chance to meet . . ."

c. As is omitted in Doct. and Disc. of Div. VII:—"offering him-selfe a lively sacrifice."

3. *Because* is replaced by *for that* in Areop.:—"For that our English will not finde letters."

CHAPTER XI.

Conclusion.

Having arrived so far, let us cast a glance back and try to repeat in conciser form the results of our examination of Milton's grammar, superficial as it has been. We have endeavoured to confine ourselves, as much as possible, to the accidence, with a view to bringing out the main differences which exist between the English of the first half of the XVIIth century, and the present state of the language. If we occasionally made a digression, devoting some space to syntactical questions, it was chiefly because the facts that gave rise to those short digressions are of a nature to strike the reader at his first perusal of Milton's prose, and to induce him to look for an explanation.

After a general survey of Milton's prose works, and a short characterisation of his style, we have attempted in our second chapter to give a short sketch of the *general state of the language at the beginning of the XVIIth century,* showing what a rapid evolution had taken place in the English tongue, and directing the attention to the first attempts made to provide the English people with rules of grammar, that might render the use of the language—spoken as well as written—simpler and easier.

The idea of introducing a phonetic writing, an idea which, strange to say, after having fallen into oblivion during centuries, is now again taking so prominent a place in the discussions of those who occupy themselves with the science of language, that idea was developed and took a form, giving rise to systems; but as each grammarian, in a narrowminded way, standing fast by his own views, refused to adopt any suggestion that might bring about a unification of those systems, moreover, as the systems themselves did not rest on a firm scientific foundation, the confusion, the unsettledness became great, and no result was arrived at.

So each writer had practically an orthography and a grammar of his own; leading writers, however, set the fashion, and an educated man like Milton was looked upon as an authority by all those who endeavoured to write and to speak correctly.

A strong tendency to simplification is to be noticed in his writings. In his *spelling,* chap. III, *he paid due attention to pronunciation as well as to etymology.* Pronunciation influenced him in the elision of weak vowels in the body and in the endings of words, chiefly of preterites and past participles of weak verbs; in the use of double consonants to indicate shortness of vowel, and in the occasional use of a "qualifying" *e* at the end of words; finally in the spelling of "vowel-sounds," chiefly in the body of words, sound ē, sound *y, ie.* Etymology strongly influenced his spelling of prefixes, and of suffixes in part.[1]

We passed on to *the verb,* chap. IV:—the use of inflections is settled in Milton:—*s (es)* is the ending of the third person sing. pres. indic.; weak verbs form their preterite and past participle quite regularly:—*(e)d, t*; a few strong verbs have retained archaic forms:—driv, sate, smit, spake.

Negative and interrogative clauses are not circumscribed, as a rule. Circumscription seems to have existed in the spoken language, but it had not found its way into written English yet.

---

[1] On Milton's orthography see:—Rost, "Die Orthographie der ersten Quarto-Ausgabe von Milton's Paradise Lost," Leipzig, 1892. The questions which we here discuss seem to have been neglected in that dissertation, or they are questions in which we have taken another range of view.

Latin influence is to be noticed in the construction of many a sentence in which the form *be* is found, where we should now use the present indicative form:—*is, are.*

Substantives are far more frequently personified than in Mn. E. prose, and, as such, are either of the masculine or of the feminine gender; this is due to Milton's poetic feeling.—The inflections are the modern ones, *s (es)*, for the plural; *s (es)*, for the Saxon genitive, the latter being appended to the noun without apostrophe. The archaic use of *his* is found in but one instance.

Adjectives are uninflected in the positive; those ending in *l* regularly double that final consonant, as sign of the length of the consonant, and at the same time of the shortness of the preceding vowel.— The German and the French comparison are indifferently used; we notice, however, a predominance of superlative forms in *est.*

Numerals, with the exception of the ordinals *fift* and *sixt,* are in form like the modern. In cumulative groups the units always come first.

Pronouns. The personal pronoun for the second person plural, nominative and oblique cases, is *ye; you* rarely occurs.— *Who* is mostly used as an interrogative pronoun, while *which* and *that* are relative. When constructed with a preposition, these pronouns are replaced by the adverb *where (there).* The influence of the Latin syntax again is felt in the very frequent occurrence of *which* with repeated antecedent. *Self,* to which a reflexive force is now attributed, was rightly regarded by Milton as a substantive, merely used to emphasize.— The reciprocal noun-pronoun *each other* is, in the two instances found, construed as in the old language, each being regarded as subject, other as object.

In chapter IX we discuss the *article,* and state that Milton is more correct in the use of definite and indefinite article *(a, an)* than his contemporaries. From the syntactical remarks we added, we drew the conclusion that Milton was quite conscious of the individualising power of the article; its omission was always the result of due reflexion.

Our last pages were devoted to the *particles;* we directed the attention to the frequent use of adjectives as adverbs, without any alteration of their form, and expressed the opinion that this was due to French influence, or to analogy with former adverbs.—Much uncertainty is to be noticed in the use of prepositions, in which Latin influence is strongly felt. Finally, we stated that the conjunction *that* was more frequently omitted than in present English; that *as* was often used to reinforce another conjunction *(when, that)*.

Thus, in the history of the English language, Milton, as a prose writer, fills a most important place, both, because, owing to his learning· and to his clear logical reasoning, he was able to bring the unsettled language to a firm basis, and because in doing this he was able to keep aloof from the mean disputes and petty rivalry which prevented the other grammarians from coming to a decisive result. To this end he arrived, not by affecting to act as a "lawgiver" on questions of grammar, but by bestowing all his care on his own spelling, accidence and syntax; so that his works might be considered as standard pieces of English, to which every one could refer. He taught by his example, and his efforts were crowned with success. His orthography and accidence do, in the main, perfectly agree with the rules now followed; where he differs, it is out of regard for the pronunciation of his time. Latin and Greek syntax strongly influence him; constructions which strike us as anomalous may always be explained by the help of similar classical ones.

Compared with his contemporaries he shows great independence in his treatment of grammar; but he contributed considerably more than they did to carry his native tongue onward, and his works are, as it were, a corner stone of "Modern English."

CONTENTS.

www.ingramcontent.com/pod-product-compliance
Lightning Source LLC
Chambersburg PA
CBHW030627270326
41927CB00007B/1339